Meditations

FROM

A PRISON CELL

Devotional Talks
From a Chinese Communist Prison

by

F. OLIN STOCKWELL

THE UPPER ROOM
The World's Most Widely Used Devotional Guide
AND
OTHER DEVOTIONAL LITERATURE
1908 Grand Avenue
Nashville 5, Tennessee

UR-80-25-954
Printed in the United States of America

To
My Gallant Comrade,
who, ignoring ancient Chinese
custom, always walks several
paces *ahead of her husband* on
The Higher Road

PREFACE

The Upper Room takes pleasure in introducing its readers to MEDITATIONS FROM A PRISON CELL by F. Olin Stockwell. It is a thrilling little volume. Dr. Stockwell had been a missionary in China for years before he was arrested by the Communists. He first sailed for China in 1929 and had been one of China's most devoted missionaries. He was arrested and put in a cell where he stayed for many months. Here he composed these meditations or devotional talks with only the help of Moffatt's translation of the New Testament. After he had written them twice in prison, they were confiscated by the Communist officials and he had to write them a third time. Fortunately the notes which he had jotted down on the borders of his New Testament were still there and he worked from them.

The Upper Room is delighted to publish these meditations. One thinks of men like John Bunyan or even the Apostle Paul as they wrote from their prison cells. Sometimes people think that the days of writing from the dungeons are past. That is not true. Here is evidence. These are eloquent testimonies to the reality of the Christian faith in these days. We recommend them heartily.

J. Manning Potts
Editor, THE UPPER ROOM
Nashville, Tennessee

Contents

Foreword

To preach from a prison cell is a high privilege not given to many. The Apostle Paul did it by preaching through the medium of his letters. His voice still reaches us across the centuries. John Bunyan did it by putting his sermon into story form that has gripped the imagination and touched the hearts of many generations. Others have done it, but they are few.

A prison cell is a superb pulpit. There all the husks of an artificial civilization are swept away. There one stands in helplessness, loneliness, and danger. There one discovers the resources of his faith and experiences in a deeper way the sustaining strength of the Everlasting Arms. There one can but speak forth the Word as he has known it himself in days of desperate need. All of this provokes a simplicity and an earnestness that is essential to any effective witness.

Moreover, preaching from a prison cell permits the unashamed use of the personal pronoun. With no reference books at hand, it is impossible to quote learned authorities. With no commentaries, one cannot elaborate as much on the meanings of Scripture passages. All one can do is to give his own personal witness—to say, "I know, for I have seen."

These devotional talks were first written during the early months of solitary imprisonment in the central police station at Chungking, West China. They were written and rewritten there. Later, they were confiscated by the Communist officials. But the ideas were jotted down on the margins of the New Testament out of which they had come. This New Testament was brought out of prison, and with its help and under God's guidance these talks have now been rewritten a third time. They are essentially as they were first noted down except for the addition of some of the verse which was composed in the same prison cell, memorized, and thus brought out.

I send these forth with the prayer that those who read them and who, perhaps, are also walking through dark places, may find it possible to transmute all their own difficulties into triumphs; that they may come to know, as I did, that God can take the worst imprisonment, even that under the Communists, and transform it into an imprisonment for Christ.

I deeply appreciate the help of my wife and that of a number of friends who have given of their advice and insight. Without their help this preaching from a Communist cell would have been lost.

Scripture passages at the beginning of the chapters and in the chapters are, unless otherwise indicated, from *The Bible: A New Translation* by James Moffatt, copyright 1935, 1953, Harper & Brothers, Publishers, and are used by permission.

F. OLIN STOCKWELL
Chicago, Illinois

Prisoner of Christ

The Lord's prisoner. —Ephesians 4:1
I whom Christ Jesus has made a prisoner. —Ephesians 3:1

MORE THAN a year had passed since that Sunday night following Thanksgiving Day when the police arrived and took me away from my wife and home. I was still in prison and had no idea when the long ordeal might end. But, as I told a Communist judge one night, the imprisonment had done two things for me—it had sharpened my understanding of communism and it had deepened my Christian faith. I discovered in prison that it was possible to transmute "prisoner of the Communists" into "prisoner of Christ."

I was a poor student, and God must have been discouraged with me more than once. But He was very patient and good beyond all telling. It was His mercy that had wrought the change.

I had my New Testament with me. On the night when I was arrested and was taken off to jail, my wife handed me my copy of Moffatt's translation of the New Testament. It was small, dog-eared, worn, and disreputable looking. When I got to jail, the guards took away my knife and razor and other things they thought I didn't need; they let me keep my New Testament. They said that it did not make any difference. But it made all the difference in the world to me. Only later, when I tried to buy the whole Bible, did I learn that the Bible was not permitted in a Communist prison. Perhaps they didn't recognize the New Testament as a part of the Bible. Or perhaps, having made a blunder in letting me keep it, they did not want to admit their mistake by taking it away. Anyway, I had it. And I used it.

On the first morning after my arrest, when I began to read the New Testament through slowly for spiritual help, I came upon those great words of Paul in which he called himself "the Lord's prisoner." I had a fellow feeling for Paul, for he was in prison when he wrote those words. His situation must have been just as hopeless as mine. But he was able to write of himself as "the Lord's prisoner," not the prisoner of Caesar. He affirmed that he

11

was one "whom Christ Jesus has made a prisoner" for the sake of others. If he could do that, I determined that I would try to do the same. I prayed to God that He would help me to accept my imprisonment not as an accident of blind fate but as a school of Christ, a way through which God could train me more effectively for His purpose.

God answered my prayer in a marvelous way. There I had time to study my New Testament. To read it by a prison window, where much of it had been written, is to see things which one never saw before. During those first months the guards were good enough to buy me paper and ink. I spent much time writing—writing devotional talks, a commentary on Matthew, Mark, and Luke, and articles about Paul and John. How I would be able to use all this material in the years ahead I did not know. Even though the guards took it up at the end of the first six months and never returned it to me, it was worthwhile.

Prayer became a richer experience in jail. I knew that friends outside were praying for me, and I was praying for myself, praying not so much that the doors would open as that God would keep me in His will. Many days were difficult. But in such times of depression, an hour of reading my New Testament and of prayer, telling God all about my heartache, loneliness, and discouragement, again opened the door to peace and contentment. Many other times the sense of God's being with me was very real and the days glowed with the light of His presence. Then I felt the overwhelming ecstasy of being alive and the thrill of all that life may mean.

What the future might hold for me, I did not know. But I believed that we do not have to be blind pawns of fate, like dumb driven cattle under the lash of careless accident. All of us are subject to unfortunate circumstances: to sickness and death, to economic collapse and betrayal of friends. Life is lived in uncertainty. At any time the cruel hand of fate may take us by the nape of the neck and thrust us behind bars of tragedy and loss.

If we can accept such misfortune and suffering as a challenge to growth, we can change them into something worthwhile.

This is not the gospel of fatalism. It is not the common Chinese attitude that faces disaster by holding up the hands and saying, "*Mo Fa!*"—"There's no help for it." Of course, many of the grim accidents of life cannot be escaped. Neither is there any explanation of why they happen, or at least, no explanation that helps us bear them.

But we may take a positive attitude toward them. We may accept them not in a spirit of resignation but in a spirit of creative venture. Through the help of God, we can believe that the jagged stones of tragedy may be built into steps leading upward to a new and wondrous tableland. We may use them to build a temple of stronger character for ourselves and a better social order for others. With the help of God, we can transmute "prisoner of the Communists" into "prisoner of Christ."

As we do so, perhaps we shall feel, as I felt then, that God has picked us out for His special blessing. Why it should have been I and not someone else whom God blessed in this way will always be a mystery to me.

> I know not why the Master's eye
> Sought me in that vast throng;
> I only know He does supply
> The grace that keeps me strong.
>
> I know not how the Master's hand
> Transformed those loaves of bread;
> I only plead my life's demand,
> And daily I am fed.
>
> I know not where the Master leads
> O'er mountain trail of pain;
> I only trust that all black seeds
> Will flower to life again.

I know not when the Master comes
To show the homeward way;
I only pray His words, "Well done!"
May crown the victory day.

Let us pray:

We thank Thee, our Father, that we are caught in the net of Thy love. As a child places his small hand in the strong hand of his father, so may we place our trust in Thee. Help us to set the sails of our faith so that every adverse wind will drive us closer to Thee. *Amen.*

God Answers Prayer

If you remain in me and my words remain in you, then ask whatever you like and you shall have it. —John 15:7

THE PROMISES of God are always conditional. The promises concerning prayer are no less conditional than others. God answers our prayers. This I found to be true in prison. But He answers only those prayers that are offered as we remain in Him and as His words and His will remain within us. Then He orders both outward events and inward spirit in harmony with His will, to the end that we may grow in grace and in knowledge of Him.

All of which means that, though God answers our prayers, He rarely answers them as we first pray them or as we, with our limited vision and selfish spirits, desire that they be answered. As a wise parent answers the insistent pleading of a child for the meat cleaver by handing him an egg-beater, so God often answers our clamouring impatience with a deeper experience of His sustaining grace.

So it was for me in prison. During those first months I prayed for an early release. It was easy to be impatient. But God did not answer my prayer by opening the doors. He answered it in other ways. The guards bought paper and ink for me. God guided me through months of searching the New Testament and in the writing of devotional talks: a commentary on the Synoptic Gospels, and articles on Paul and John. Often I came to the end of one bit of work with no clear idea as to what I could do next. But the next day God would guide me into some other line of thought or activity that was productive of good. Thus, God answered my need in these creative ways.

The most difficult period was during the first summer when I had nothing at all to read for a time, having loaned my New Testament to a fellow-prisoner in the next room. As a result I felt I had nothing to do. Then God opened up a new door to me, the door of poesy. I wrote verse all summer long. The days were hot, the food poor, and the nights were harried with bedbugs and noise. No beauty, friendship, books, music, or freedom were there. But God lifted me out of those heat-burdened, weary days and put my feet upon a mountain top by pouring poetry into my soul. At the end of the summer, I looked back with amazement upon one of the most creative and joyful experiences I had ever known. I thanked God that He had answered my prayers not by delivering me *from jail,* as He had Peter, but by delivering me *in jail,* as He had Paul. I knew then how Paul in Rome was able to write his most joyful letter from a prison cell. I had found the same joy in prison, too.

At the end of the first year, when I had hoped to be released, God did not open the doors, but He did inspire me to write the story of my imprisonment on the margins of an anthology of poetry. Acquired after the first summer of my imprisonment, this was the only book I had other than my New Testament. I found joy in writing my experience, hoping to help others understand what had happened to me and to China. For some strange reason, the officials never opened that anthology of poetry. They did not know that the story was written on its margins. When I was transferred to the prison for counter-revolutionaries, the guards never opened that book in which the story was written. Whether or not I would get it out of China I did not know. But I lived from day to day in the confidence that this problem, as the problem of my eventual release, was in God's hands and not mine. So I was at peace.

As I look back over the months that I spent in prison, I am amazed at the way in which God answered my prayers. It seems to be that every refusal of God to give me what I prayed for was not an outright refusal of what I asked but was aways a substitution of something better. I prayed for more books for reading; God answered me by leading me to do more writing. I prayed for a hymnal; God answered me by quickening my memory of hymns which I had learned before. I prayed for an open door to freedom; God answered me by freeing my spirit through writing poetry. I prayed for some way to make that experience creative for others; God answered by guiding me to write my story.

The days in the second prison were not easy. The constant insistence that I see all questions through Communist eyes, the distorting of all facts to fit into the concrete forms of Communist ideology, the hammering of half-truths into the all-truth of communism was a process which wore on my nerves and made me long for solitary confinement again. But even then I found that if I remained in God and His will remained within me, that if I left all things in His hands, my prayer for patience and courage to meet each day was wondrously answered.

This long experience convinced me that God does answer our prayers in ways far more wonderful than we think possible. But His answer is always in harmony with our deepest need and to the end that we may become more truly sons and daughters of His. Only as we remain in Him and only as His words and His will remain in us can we see our prayers bearing fruit in transformed lives.

> God answers prayer!
> Not as a pinching miser would,
> Weighing out each ounce of food

On skimpy scale, for fear he should
Turn gain to loss in surly mood;
But grants us all we ask and more,
Poured forth in love from His rich store.

God answers prayer!
But not in ways that we would mark.
For, like Saint Paul, we oft would start
For Rome, to end in dungeons dark.
But if in trust, we lose not heart,
By faith and hope and love begird,
With greater power we preach God's Word.

God answers prayer!
Denying all in tears we ask,
And calling us to sterner task;
To drain pain's cup, a bitter flask,
As held by love in tragic mask,
He turns to joy our sorest loss,
Redeems again the blood-stained cross.

Let us pray:

We rejoice, O God, that our prayers are not always answered as we pray them. We pray so foolishly. We would seek ease, pleasure, quick results, and freedom from pain. We would live in a hot-house protected from all inclement weather. But Thou knowest best. Answer Thou not the superficial prayers of our lips, but the hunger of our lives, that, no matter what the cost, we may grow into spiritual fellowship with Thee. *Amen.*

The Way of the Blessed

Blessed are those. . . . —Matthew 5:3

IN PRE-REVOLUTIONARY China the New Year season was a period of great rejoicing and merry-making. The houses were decorated for the occasion. Among the many streamers that were pasted over the doorways, one of the most popular was the wish that the occupants might have much of the "three blesseds." Those "blesseds," as everyone knew, were long life, much wealth, and many children.

The "blesseds" which Jesus talks about move upon quite a different plane. There are eight of them, and they may be divided into two groups.

The first four are those *who feel poor in spirit, the mourners, the humble,* and those *who hunger and thirst for goodness.* This is a strange group that Jesus called "blessed" or happy. Who are they? Why, they are those who have been beaten down by life until they have nothing to boast about. Therefore, they are humble and meek. They are those who mourn for themselves or for others. They are those who are in a state of moral collapse and long for nothing quite so much as goodness.

In other words, these first four groups who are blessed are those who have reached the end of their resources and have come to realize their own helplessness. Knowing this, they can do but one thing—cry out to God for His sustaining mercy and grace. When they do this, God's grace comes in as surely as the tide sweeps in and lifts the boats along the shore, for God cannot take hold until we let go.

The second group of blessed ones are the *merciful, the pure in heart* (who are really the loving in heart, the perfect ones who love even their enemies), and those who are *peacemakers* even though they are persecuted for it. Who are these? These are they who in the spirit of Christ have gone out to build a new world. They have been defeated on the battlefield and cast out, as our missionaries have been cast out of China or as many of our Chinese co-workers are suffering there today. They thus reach the same place as the first group, the place where they realize their own helplessness and inadequacy. They can do nothing other than to surrender to God with a new and deeper completeness. As they cast

18

themselves upon God, God's grace takes hold. They have joined the fellowship of the defeated. In this fellowship they find new and deeper joy, for it is here that the grace of God is known in all its wonder.

God cannot come into our souls until we ourselves open the doors and let Him in. When life is easy for us and we have no problems we cannot solve ourselves or when our bank accounts are adequate and all material needs are met, often we feel no deep need of God. But when life tumbles in, when tragedy stalks in and grips us by the throat, then we know our own helplessness. We cry out to God. And then it is that the grace of God becomes known to us. It is known to us only in proportion to our sense of felt need.

I saw this truth clearly for the first time there in prison. For the first time I really knew what Jesus meant by this strange list of "blesseds." My own experience opened my eyes to the meaning of the Scriptures.

How different these "blesseds" are from those which the Chinese talk about at New Year's time. Long life, much wealth, and many children—probably most of us would be ready to settle for these, for most of us hardly know what Jesus is talking about. This shows how little we understand the way of Christ.

This joy that Jesus is talking about is open to all. Very few can have children and wealth and long life. There just isn't enough money to go around so that everyone can live in luxury. More than half the world still goes to bed hungry every night. But the joy that springs from a sense of God's presence and power is open to everyone.

This happiness that Jesus spoke of is not subject to the accidents and vicissitudes of life. Indeed, the more unfortunate you may be in material things, the more surely you may cast yourself upon Him. With the Chinese "blesseds" it is quite the contrary. When a revolution sweeps across the country, those who have wealth, power, influence are caught up and blown away in its typhoon. Those who were in power one day were with me in prison the next.

The blessedness of which Jesus spoke lasts. Even if a man be lucky and gain wealth, it is often dissipated by the next generation. Even if he has many children, they are often a disappointment and a heartache. Even if he lives to an old age, the later years are weighted with weakness and ill health and may turn sour on the tongue. But this is not true with the grace of God. God's grace lasts. It lasts not only through life, turning the sunset years into years of radiant glory, but even holds the promise of fellowship and increased joy and growth in the land of eternal day.

All of this may sound strange to you, but it is marvelously true. The way to real victory is the way of surrender to God. My own experience is no different from that of scores of other missionaries and Chinese friends who have been caught under the sharp harrow of a Communist dictatorship. God was able to change days of uncertainty, loneliness, suffering, and defeat into joy, peace, and patience. As I prayed that His will might be my will and as I sought to put all the issues of the hour into His hands, I found a joy that passed all understanding. It is the way of the blessed open to you and to me in every hour of need.

Let us pray:

It is difficult, our Father, to pray for defeat. All our strident pride, selfishness, and insistent ego cry out against it. We want our way, not Thy way. But when we get our way, life turns sour on the tongue. Forgive us, we pray. Compel us, at whatever cost, to bow under Thy yoke. Only then shall we find an inner peace, that true blessedness that endures. *Amen.*

20

Help Me to Forgive!

Forgive us our debts as we ourselves have forgiven our debtors.
—Matthew 6:12

ONE OF the doors through which the grace of God comes into our lives is the door of complete surrender. Another door is that of forgiveness of others.

Jesus has placed this teaching at the heart of the prayer which He taught His disciples. It is the only conditional petition in that prayer. We pray that God will forgive us *as*—or *in so far as*—we forgive those who have wronged us. And then, as if to underline it, Jesus warns, "If you do not forgive men, your Father will not forgive your trespasses either." This is the highest peak of all of the teachings of Jesus; It is the highest insight of any religion anywhere. It is the clear recognition of the fact that God's grace is available to us only as we are in right relation with our fellow men.

I faced that condition when I first went into prison. During those first days, when I felt so keenly the need of God's sustaining grace, I knew that I had to take Jesus literally. I had to meet this condition. I had to forgive.

It was not easy. I knew that I had been railroaded into prison. I was put in prison because of the Korean War. I had had nothing to do with the war. But it had built up the prejudices and hates in China that put me into jail. I was in prison because of an unfortunate school situation in which a number of Communist teachers and students had been injured. Those who were to blame for the situation had moved away before I moved to that school. I had had nothing to do with the school or the problems involved until just before the Communist government came in. Then all the blame of the past years was loaded on to my shoulders. That was one reason I was in jail. I was in jail for another reason; I had handled American relief supplies, trying to help the Chinese people. Because of this, I was an "imperialist." So I could have spent those early weeks in prison chewing my fingernails and nursing hate and malice against all those who put me there. Thus, I could have turned my prison cell into a veritable hell. I knew hate was a dead-end road. It is always a dead-end road.

I took Jesus quite literally. I knelt down and prayed that God would take all hatred out of my heart, that He would help me to pray for those who are guiding China's destiny, to pray for the officials and guards who have charge over me, and to pray for those who were bearing false witness against me. As I thus prayed, all the hate and malice flowed out; joy, peace, courage, patience, and power came in. I had opened the door to God's grace. Until I had done that, God could do nothing for me. When I did open the door, everything changed.

One day I read a speech by Lenin. The only literature we had in prison was Communist literature, speeches by Lenin, Stalin, Mao Tzetung, and other Communist writers. Lenin was condemning those who took the pacifist position by pointing out the inconsistencies in it and its ineffectiveness to build a new world. He wrote something like this, "If I were a mother and had a small son, I would take him into my arms and say, 'My boy, grow strong, grow fast. And when you grow up, learn to shoot and shoot straight. Then the time will come when you can seize a gun and shoot down all who oppress the great laboring class. You can win your own and others' freedom only through hate and violence and bloodshed.' "

This is the way of death, the gospel according to Hitler, Mussolini, Lenin, Stalin, and countless numbers of dictators who have blackened the pages of history with their crimes. It is the way of death for society no less than for the individual. The way of love, the way of forgiveness, is not alien to life; it is the way, and the only way, to life.

But if your experience is like mine, you do not find forgiveness easy. Yet God demands that we forgive. So if we ask for His help, God gives of His Spirit to us that we may forgive. "The Spirit assists us in our weakness; for we do not know how to pray aright." The full grace of God cannot come into our hearts until we unlock the door of love. But enough of God's grace is available to help us turn the key to unlock our hearts if we are willing to acknowledge our need, if we but pray, "O God, help me forgive!"

> O God, teach me to forgive!
> Else with myself I cannot live.
> Black hate will poison life,
> Blur the truth with rancor rife,
> Create within a fruitless strife.
> Pray Thee, wield Thy surgeon's knife!
> O God, help me forgive!
>
> O God, teach me to forgive!
> Else with others I cannot live.
> Sowing bitterness and pain,
> Disgracing Thy dear Body's name,
> Blind to sin's dark, widening stain—
> Pray Thee, my proud heart reclaim!
> O God, help me forgive!
>
> O God, teach me to forgive!
> Else with Thee I cannot live.
> For until from malice free
> My Master's face I cannot see,
> Nor His disciple claim to be.
> Pray Thee, guide to Calvary!
> O God, help me forgive!

Let us pray:

It is easy to pray for Thy forgiveness, our Father. Thou art love and understanding. Thou art infinite, and we are finite. But to forgive one of our fellows, or to ask another's forgiveness for wrongs that we have done—that is difficult. It is the price of Christian discipleship. Help us, our Father, to pay that price in humility and in joy. *Amen.*

Abolishing Anxiety

Never be anxious, but always make your requests known to God in prayer and supplication with thanksgiving; so shall God's peace, that surpasses all our dreams, keep guard over your hearts and minds in Christ Jesus. —Philippians 4:6, 7

NO WORDS from the New Testament meant more to me during those months of imprisonment than these. I discovered them quite early. I took hold of them like a drowning man grasping at a piece of driftwood, and I held on. I found them wondrously true.

These words were written in prison, written by Paul while he was waiting in uncertainty, an uncertainty which was as galling as his chains. They were written out of a lifetime of experience, an experience of which he speaks only once in his letters. Then he wrote, "I have been often at the point of death; five times have I had forty lashes . . . , three times I have been beaten by the Romans, once pelted with stones, three times shipwrecked, adrift at sea for a whole night and day; I have been often on my travels, I have been in danger from rivers and robbers, in danger from Jews and Gentiles, through dangers of town and of desert, through dangers of the sea, through dangers among false brothers—through labor and hardship, through many a sleepless night, through hunger and thirst, starving many a time, cold and ill-clad, and all the rest of it." After these lines were written, Paul suffered another mobbing, a shipwreck, and at least three years of indeterminate waiting in jail. Out of it all he could write, "Never be anxious." Such a bugle call to courage and faith meant much to me during my imprisonment.

But I found that I had to do exactly what Paul says. He says that we are to make our requests known to God *with thanksgiving*. Anxiety's antitoxin is thanksgiving. By beginning with thanksgiving, we have some hope of defeating the enemy.

Thanksgiving puts our worries in their right perspective. Through thanking God for all that He has done for us in the past, we can know that He is in control. We can look back over the years, as can every other pilgrim of the Way, and remember the many times when God has brought victory out of defeat and courage out of despair. . . . If such were true then, surely it can be true now. Our affairs are in His hands.

I kept trying to maintain this attitude over the first year. Later, I was transferred to the prison for counter-revolutionaries where I lived in a ten-foot square room with seven other prisoners, all of whom were Chinese. They had been given the task by the government of changing my mind and attitude. They railed away at me for ten or twelve hours day after day. When I woke up one morning, a prisoner asked, "How did you sleep last night?" My answer was, "I slept fine." He said, "That's queer. Every one of us who has come here could neither sleep nor eat for two or three weeks until we had confessed all our crimes and cleared our case with the government. We had too many worries and fears. But you are normal. You sleep and eat like a pig. There is something the matter with you." I could not tell him that I left it in God's hands, but that was true. If God could see me through fourteen months of solitary imprisonment, keeping me sane and happy, He could certainly see me through the rest of it. I gave God thanks for the past; He gave me courage for the present.

So Paul tells us to make our requests known *with thanksgiving*. As we do that, God steps into the center of our thought. We know His power now. We remember how He has delivered us in the past.

Then something wonderful happens, or at least it happened to me. I believe that it can happen to you. As I told God of my problems and sought His aid—in thanksgiving—the peace of God, like a stalwart sentinel, moved in to keep guard over my heart and mind, over my emotions and thoughts, to keep them *in Christ Jesus*. It was not easy, but it was possible. I had to keep praying, keep my thoughts upon God and continue to trust Him, or I found myself slipping back into that dreary round of worry about problems I could not solve and fears of a future I could not fathom. But as I held on in prayer, with thanksgiving, anxiety loosened its cold grip upon my heart and I fell asleep in peace.

Did my fellow-prisoners guess the secret of my serenity? I dared not ask them. I had been warned that all discussion about religion and all practice of prayer were forbidden. I continued to thank God that no one could enforce a ban on prayer or prevent the peace of God from keeping guard over heart and mind.

We thank Thee, Lord, for prayer.
For when we're least aware
Cold fog, without a sound,
Creeps in and wraps us 'round,
To crush the soul's rebound.
We kneel to Thee to pray;
Thy sun drives fog away.

We thank Thee, Lord, for prayer.
When we no longer dare
To face the wave's chill scorn,
Our sails all tattered, torn,
Our hands all battered, worn,
We kneel to Thee to pray;
Thy help is ours straightway.

We thank Thee, Lord, for prayer.
When in our dark despair
The day fades into night,
And clouds obscure all light,
Till eyes are robbed of sight
To tell the wrong from right,
We kneel to Thee to pray;
And night turns into day.

Let us pray:

Forgive us, Father, for not trusting Thee. We say words, shallow, perfunctory, insincere. But we do not believe them. We call Thee

26

Father, but we do not trust Thee in childlike simplicity and sincerity. Forgive Thou us. Grant us a new understanding of Thy way for us and a deeper willingness to surrender all things to Thee. *Amen.*

The Light of the World

Ye are the light of the world. —Matthew 5:14

IN PRISON this verse impressed me as about the most absurd statement that Jesus ever made. How absurd to tell me that I was the light of the world: *I*, who could look back upon years of blundering and sinning and failing; *I*, who was just a prisoner of the Communist with little or no hope of being able again to "speak a good word for Jesus Christ." If I had said that Jesus did not say this to me, but said it to a group of fishermen along a Galilean shore, it would be about the same thing. Certainly they, with their lack of experience, their failures, and their sin were little different from me.

It is easy to think of *Jesus* as the light of the world. He speaks of Himself as such in John's Gospel. He is so named in Holman Hunt's great picture of a thorn-crowned king standing with lighted lantern before a closed and vine-covered door. We sing, "The light of the world is Jesus." But here He does not speak of Himself, but of you and I—we are the light of the world. To take this seriously makes a lot of difference.

We are not responsible for the size of our light. Each of us has a different wattage, some twenty, some thirty, some sixty. God determines the wattage. But we determine the voltage. If we burn our full candle power, we must keep our contacts clean, tight, and strong.

It is easy to think that our wattage is so small that whether we burn or not makes little difference. But when we burn together, it makes a tremendous difference. Some years ago I was at Soldier Field in Chicago where a great crowd had gathered. It was night time. The director of the program asked everyone to get a match or cigarette lighter ready. All the lights were turned off; it was very dark. He then said, "Now all light your matches together." All of us followed his instruction, and the field became very light again. Alone, a single match does not matter, but together they light up the world.

We shine in different ways. Some have made their lights to shine through the books they have written. Harriet Beecher Stowe wrote her *Uncle Tom's Cabin,* and men came to look upon slavery with new eyes and rose to destroy it forever. Upton Sinclair cast light upon many dark places in American life, upon the meat-packing industry, newspaper publishing, and the liquor traffic. John Steinbeck wrote his book about the itinerant wage earner in the fields and orchards of California. A more recent book has cast light upon our public institutions for the mentally ill. None of these books show a balanced view of the whole picture. They are torchlights casting their gleam only upon some dark area of American life and thus helping us to see what we had not seen before. As such, they have their worth.

Other persons shine not through books they have written but through lives they have lived. Each mission field has its list of heroes, men and women who have lived their lives in needy places. By their gallantry, love, and insight into the needs of the country in which they have worked, these people have helped to shed light in dark places. Some of these we know about; most of them are nameless. Not only these, but many other thousands today in quiet and unnoticed places behind "iron curtains," created by dictatorships, are continuing to let their lights shine for God.

Often these lights shine where you least expect them. A few years ago, we spent our summer on one of the foothills of Omei Mountain, one of the several sacred mountains of China located out in the west. As we climbed the winding path to the top of this sacred mountain, we came to the Twin Waterfalls, a beautiful spot of singing water ringed with graceful bamboos. There beside the mountain path was a little house in which a Christian woman, Mrs. Chiang lived. She had a small crèche for unwanted babies. Any mountain family who had found the struggle for existence too grim could leave an unwanted infant at the door of this cottage. Mrs. Chiang would receive the child and nurse it back to health. Then she would find a home for it somewhere on the plain below, a home in which the baby would be welcome and would be given a chance for normal childhood. No foreign money was behind this program of service. Back of it were only sacrifice, love, and a determination to help others, expressed by a single Christian woman who had herself walked through dark places.

So all of us can and must shine if we are to be "the light of the world." As lights we must light up the need of the world and show that the love of God in Christ Jesus alone can meet that need. Then men, seeing our good works, will not praise us but our "Father in heaven."

> Light of our dark lives,
> Set our hearts aflame,
> For all our light derives
> Its brilliance from Thy name.
> Then shall all men see
> The light that streams from Thee.
>
> Thou whom all men see,
> A city on a hill,
> Help us to learn of Thee,
> Eager to do Thy will,
> To hold Thy banner high
> Before each passer-by.
>
> We cannot climb alone
> The path to shining peak;
> Our weakness we must own,

Thy wondrous power we seek.
We only mount above
When held by Thy sure love.

Let us pray:

O Thou God of great expectancy, how often we fail Thee. When we should glow with truth and love and hope, we allow the fickle winds of praise or blame, of pride or fear to blow out our candle of Christian witness. O Thou God of undiscouraged love, forsake us not. In Thy light may we see light and share that light with others. *Amen.*

Washing Feet

You are bound to wash one another's feet. —John 13:14

I WENT to bed one night thinking about this incident of Jesus' washing the feet of His disciples. I woke up long before day with the following lines forming themselves in my mind. I wrote them down, then memorized them, and have repeated them again and again.

"But washing feet is an onerous task!
Really more than He ought to ask;
Have to remove your coat and vest,
Down on your knees at His behest.

"Why don't people wash their own?
'Twould be much simpler to do it alone.
Of course, there're some who haven't the strength,
But they could learn somehow, at length.

"Why did they walk in dust and mire?
There're plenty of paths a little higher.
It isn't fair that we should suffer
For every ignorant, careless duffer.

30

"Surely there's an easier way—
Each give a quarter, enough to pay
A strong, efficient, and willing hand,
Specially trained for this demand."

So the disciples, surly, mutter
Thoughts they fear aloud to utter.
Soft as the breeze the Master sighed,
"But I for you was crucified."

Whether or not the disciples felt and talked like this, I do not know. But *we* certainly talk this way. We become impatient with the slowness of personal service. We want some wholesale, immediate, and efficient plan for saving the world. We vote our millions for relief and rehabilitation and are surprised that they win us few friends. We raise our quota for university buildings, hospitals, and other projects and are surprised at the slowness with which they result in converting another country. We want to do our "Christian duty" by helping but we want to do it at a distance with as little touch with those whom we help as possible. We would like to be Christian missionaries—*in absentia.*

My neighbor in prison had body lice. I loaned him my blanket one day; then I had lice, too. If I had just been farther away, I would not have caught his lice, and he would not have had my blanket. Christian faith, like body lice, cannot be caught except by contact. Other people will never understand our Christian faith until we get close enough to wash their feet, to share in that personal service through which the spirit of Christ can shine.

At first thought, this seems a terribly slow and costly way to preach the gospel. We have so many other ways—radios, newspapers, books, movies, and other mediums through which we can reach so many more people at one time. All of these are worthwhile, but they do not take the place of the intimate, personal relationship in which personalities grow. For the Christian faith is not only taught; it must also be caught.

This method of proclaiming the Christian gospel is not as slow as we may first think. The influence of one life reaches out in ever widening circles until it touches far more than we can see.

During the war against Japan, one of the top generals in China told of being in Hankow during an air raid. He heard the Japanese planes coming over and heard bombs dropping. Then he looked out of his hotel window to see what part of the city might be in flames. Much to his surprise, he saw an ambulance already speeding by on its mission of mercy. Others had not yet dared venture out. But that ambulance from a Christian hospital, manned by Christian personnel, both foreign and Chinese, was on its way. Such passion for personal service so impressed the general that he told about it to many an audience, inspiring others to go and do likewise.

During that same period, Doctor Bethune, a Canadian surgeon, was working in North China in the territory occupied by the Eighth Route Army. He was not a Communist in his thinking. He was simply motivated by a Christian passion to serve where the need was greatest. He toiled in that needy area, giving his skill to the last full measure of devotion. He died there in the midst of his task. His life of unselfish service impressed the Communists so much that today they have erected a Bethune Hospital in his memory. His life reached out to inspire and guide others far beyond anything he dreamed possible.

So we might cite example after example of the influence of those who have stooped to "wash one another's feet," who have witnessed to their inner faith through outward personal service. The total impact of such personal services is doing far more than anyone can dream in welding those invisible chains of understanding and goodwill that hold our world together.

All of this contributes not only to the creation of the kingdom of God but also to the increasing joy of the doer.

Bishop W. Y. Chen often told about a friend who came to his door in those early months of the Japanese war. His friend came with a heavy burden on his heart, for he had lost everything. His two oldest sons had been seized and taken away by the Japanese never to be heard of again. A bomb had struck his little home on the outskirts of Shanghai, killing his wife and three younger children. He was distraught with grief and did not know what to do. Bishop Chen invited him into his house. They had a talk together, read a portion of the New Testament, and had prayer. In fellowship and prayer the stricken man found peace. But he felt that he must find something to do or he would go mad. So Bishop Chen took him out to one of the orphan camps in Shanghai, a place where boys and girls who had been orphaned by the war were gathered together for temporary shelter and care. This man took charge of the orphan camp. He threw himself into the care of those helpless boys and girls. When Bishop Chen visited him there a few weeks later, he found a man surrounded by a score of children who called him, "Daddy," a man who had found peace and joy again. He said, "I was robbed of my wife and five children, but God has given me more than a hundred children. It is wonderful to be in this place."

He had found, as many another Christian disciple has found, that the way of personal service to others is the way of joy and developing life.

Let us pray:

Deliver us, O God, from spiritual blindness. Correct Thou our vision that we may see Thee in the love that sanctifies the daily round and the common task. May Thy life shine through our lives until we shall seek to express Thy spirit in every word and deed, every attitude and thought of the day. Grant unto us the mind of the Lord Jesus. *Amen.*

The Providence of God

My God will supply all your own needs from his wealth in Glory in Christ Jesus. —Philippians 4:19

A CHRISTIAN dwells in a world of providential care. He lives in the faith that, whatever may happen, God will never forsake him.

This providence of God may be seen in outward events. The doors *do* open for Peter. Our loved one *is* healed of disease and restored to life and health again. A letter *does* come in the mail with a check in it to meet our desperate need. The sea of difficulty and discouragement *is* rolled back as if by the hand of God and we walk across on dry land. These things do happen. At the time we often do not realize that they are the providence of God.

Finding it impossible to do any creative work after the Communists came in, we asked for a permit to leave China. We then waited impatiently for several months. Packing my books and getting many of them off by mail to Hong Kong, cleaning the attic of an accumulation of junk, selling our victrola records and piano, and getting my watch repaired—all these and other activities were, as far as I knew then, only preparation for our departure from China. But later in prison, as I looked back upon them and realized their relation to my imprisonment, I saw them as the providence of God. Like a mountain climber, we trudge wearily up a winding, stony path with no clear vision of whence we came or whither we go. But times are provided when, on some peak or through some break in the trees, we can trace the winding trail through the mists below. Even so, to most of us there come those times when, if we pause and look back over the years, we can trace in some event, in some good fortune, or even in some accident which looked wholly tragic at the time, ways in which God has led us. Like Jacob of old we may say, "The Eternal must be here, and I never knew it."

But we must not limit the providence of God to outward events. God delivered Peter *from* prison, but He sustained Paul *in* prison.

34

This sustaining power was so real to Paul that though in chains in prison he could write a joyful letter assuring the church at Philippi that his "affairs have really tended to advance the gospel." Then he could close the letter with the confident assertion, "My God will supply all your own needs from his wealth in Glory in Christ Jesus." This providence of God is known to us, also, in our imprisonments.

It is this overshadowing presence of God that can keep us from worry, give us courage, and help us to interpret our difficulties as opportunities for growth. In other words, this providence may guide our thoughts in the most difficult and pressing problem we face. While living through those months of solitude, I often prayed:

> Guide Thou my thoughts lest they should stray
> To tortuous paths in sin's dark wood,
> Where sordid lusts and passions' mood
> In thickets hide from light of day;
> To deep ravines of bitter hate,
> Of jealous care and chilling fear,
> Of wounded pride and lies that sear—
> O, save Thou me from such dire fate!
>
> Guide Thou my thoughts that they may stay
> On sunny shores of laughter strong,
> Where friends and beauty join in song
> Their children fair in care-free play;
> Or climb where singing breezes sigh
> Through fragrant pines of faith and hope,
> Still marching up o'er green-gowned slope
> To God's great peaks against the sky.

This prayer, or some prayer like it, must also have been on the lips of Paul. Writing to the church at Philippi, he closes with a great word, "Finally, brothers, keep in mind whatever is true, whatever is worthy, whatever is just, whatever is pure."

Thus, the miracles of God are of two types, those that are wrought in outward events and those that effect an inner change. Unless the outward event creates an inner change, it is really no miracle in the New Testament sense. A miracle is that event, either outward or inward, which convinces the participant that God is alive, active, and over-ruling in His providential care. A missionary was caught by bandits some years ago in South China and was held for several days in a small mountain fortress. One night, one of the guards came, opened the door, and urged him to flee. To the missionary that escape was the providence of God. It was hardly that to his captors. John reports that when God spoke to Jesus some said it was the voice of the Divine, while others simply thought it had thundered. A miracle is never a supernatural event to one who is spiritually blind and deaf.

In prison I was grateful to God for those things which made it easier for me. But most of all I praised Him for the miracle within, the knowledge that He never left me alone.

> We praise Thee, Lord, that Thou didst still
> The raging storm on Galilee;
> But praise Thee more that Thou canst fill
> With courage hearts that rest in Thee.
>
> We praise Thee, Lord, that Thou didst heal
> The lame with such forgiving grace;
> But praise Thee more that we may feel
> The cleansing love of Thy dear face.
>
> We praise Thee, Lord, that One arose
> From guarded tomb on Easter Day;
> Still from that empty grave there flows
> New hope to all who walk Thy way.

Let us pray:

We thank Thee, Father, that Thou art not imprisoned in the pages of a dead past. We thank Thee that we may still see Thee in a cloud by day and a pillar of fire by night, guiding us across the trackless sands of this life. Open our ears to Thy voice! Alert us to Thy presence! Help us to be aware of Thy miracle-working power in every redemptive event, in every discovery of truth, in every spiritual victory today. *Amen.*

The Higher Path

To show you a still higher path. —I Corinthians 12:31

THESE ARE the words Paul used to introduce his poem on love in the thirteenth chapter of First Corinthians. He announces that he is going to show them a better way, a "higher path." It is the same "path" which Jesus talks about in the Sermon on the Mount. Paul had learned it from Jesus.

In contrast to the rule by which most of us live, "An eye for an eye and a tooth for a tooth," Jesus set forth the rule of aggressive, undiscouraged goodwill. If someone strikes us on one cheek, we are to turn to him the other. If a braggart soldier forces us at gun-point to carry his load for him one mile, we are to do it cheerfully, even being willing to carry it two. We are to love our enemies because that is what God does. For God makes His sun to "rise on the evil and the good, and sends rain on the just and the unjust." We are to be perfect not in knowledge or in power but in love, as our "heavenly Father is perfect" in love. This is the "still higher path."

As I read the Gospels in prison, it seemed to me that this was not primarily a teaching on international relations, a pacifist program laid down to end all wars. Neither did it seem primarily a teaching relative to industrial or social conflict. Rather, Jesus seemed to be talking to you and to me about ourselves, about the way in which we should live from day to day.

Jesus is saying that the way of aggressive goodwill, of undiscouraged forgiveness, is the only way to emotional maturity. To nurse a grudge against someone else, to carry malice and ill will, is to create emotional tensions which tear life to pieces. For a child to give way to emotional tantrums can be understood and in some measure forgiven. But for an adult to erupt like a volcano is different. He should have already grown up emotionally.

During the Second World War the Germans used the magnetic mine, a devilish device which was set off by the accumulated magnetism of a ship at sea. But a German, named Karl F. Gauss, discovered a way of demagnetizing the ship, draining off its surplus magnetic energy before it left port, thus making it impervious to the magnetic mine. Most of us need something to drain off our surplus emotional load. Someone says something we don't like. We imagine others are against us. We worry about it. We brood upon it. Emotional tensions increase. Our sleep is broken. Food becomes tasteless. We cannot get it off our minds. Something happens and we go off like an exploded mine, creating havoc on all sides. We need some way to lessen our emotional tension and give us peace. Jesus says that the only way out is forgiveness. An undiscouraged goodwill is the road to emotional maturity.

Positive goodwill is the only way to fellowship, to getting along with others. That is true in the average community or church where all of us, being human, do things and say things which offend others. It was true there in prison. The guards were often sharp, censorious, demanding. The officials rarely, if ever, smiled at one of us prisoners. We were supposed to have committed crimes against "the people," and the officials represented "the people" in their hatred of us and our crimes. No laughter was there. To react to all of this in a perfectly normal way with hatred and bitterness was to increase one's difficulties. The man across the hall did that, and he wore clanking chains and handcuffs day and night. In that

Communist prison, as in the world outside, the only way of "getting along" with people was the way of positive goodwill.

Postive goodwill is the way to God, for it is God's way and not man's. Man says, "Hate!" God says, "Love!"

Peter came to Jesus once with the question as to whether forgiving another as many as seven times would be enough. Jesus answered, "Seven times? I say, seventy times seven!" This really means unlimited forgiveness. If you would forgive four hundred and ninety times, by then you would have got the habit of forgiving and just would not stop.

This so amazed Peter that Jesus told him the story of a king who forgave his steward three million pounds, a huge debt which the steward could not pay. Then this steward found a servant who owed him only twenty pounds. He became angry and had the servant thrown into prison for his debt. When the king heard of how his steward had acted, he was very angry. He had forgiven him of a three million pound debt, but the steward would not forgive another person a miserable twenty pounds.

Is this the way it looks to God? Is this the way it would look to us if we were to see it through God's eyes? Only as we realize what God has done and is doing for us, only as we see His love revealed to us in the life and death of His Son, our Lord Jesus Christ—only then can we realize that our pettiness and meanness, our selfishness and hate are closing the door to Him. Only as we know that He has forgiven us of three million pounds can we forgive others their paltry twenty pounds.

Let us pray:

We stand before Thy cross, O Christ, in deep humility and need. Thy love that forgives to the uttermost shames our petty pride and miserable malice. We see our shabby selfishness and chilling bitterness in all their stark reality. Before Thy cross, we see ourselves, and we loathe what we see. O Christ, grant us Thy forgiveness in proportion to our need, and set us afire with a love that burns out all hate and prejudice and gnawing ill will. Help us to follow Thee even to Golgotha. *Amen.*

God-Guided Pain

The pain God is allowed to guide. —II Corinthians 7:10

TO SAY that pain is *universal* is to say something we all know. Suffering, tragedy, pain, and sorrow are the lot of men in every clime and in every generation.

To say that we do not know the *why* of pain is also to repeat a well-known fact. One book in the Bible, the book of Job, struggles with the problem but finds no solution to it. Turning to the New Testament, we likewise find the search for an answer to the riddle of human suffering a difficult one. But the New Testament goes far beyond the Old Testament in telling us how to use suffering. We do not know what electricity is, but we have learned how to use it. So pain, though a mystery, may be used. The New Testament says that it may be used for growth of Christian character, for a closer fellowship with Christ, and for the redemption of the world.

During the summer months of my first year in prison, I wrote the following verse "To One Who Waits." I thought of my wife waiting for me on the outside, perhaps in Chungking, perhaps in Hong Kong, perhaps at home in America. Wherever she might be, I thought of her waiting without any word as to where I was or how I was getting along. I hoped and prayed that the whole experience of long and uncertain waiting might be creative for her. I phrased my hope and prayer thus:

> For this sour soil of folly and sin
> To grow such thorny, twisted tree
> Of wasted months creates within
> A brackish taste.
> Also I see,

40

Its bitter fruit pressed to lips
I love, and held by ruthless fate
And loyalty's hand until last sips
Drain the glass of wordless wait.
Can this bitter draught give strength
Or nerve you to unflagging zeal?
Can you use such fruit at length
Your own and others' pain to heal?
Do we hear the Master's tone
Bidding us walk, as He, alone?

The last six lines of this verse pose the three questions that from a Christian viewpoint are central to suffering. They suggest that suffering may be used to strengthen our own devotion, that through it we may find comfort for ourselves and others, and that in it we may experience a deeper fellowship with Christ.

A few months before my arrest, I talked with a missionary friend who had received a very strange letter. He had written to a Chinese Christian layman away up in a village in Northwest China. He asked this friend how he and his church fellowship were getting along. The reply that my friend received read like this: "Dear Brother, we received your letter. But we do not read the Bible any more, for that is superstition. We do not attend church any more, for that is worn-out custom. We do not believe in religion, because that also is a decadent superstition. Thank you for your letter. Sincerely yours," and signed. But at the bottom of the letter was one great word, "Emmanuel." My friend understood. He knew that Christian layman did not dare write freely, for he would get both himself and his Christian group into trouble. So he wrote what the Communist censor in the post-office would want to read. But at the bottom of the letter he added, "Emmanuel," —"God is with us."—This word the Communist censor would not understand, but it would express the truth of the situation. In all their trials they knew, as I knew, that God was with them.

41

Under suffering, trial, and persecution real faith is deepened and strengthened because God is in it, guiding it to His own ends.

God is the one who comforts us and makes it possible for us to comfort others. This had become so real to Paul that he could write the church at Corinth that he thanked God for his sufferings. Through his suffering he had come to know the comfort of God, a comfort which he could share with others. He never defines this comfort, but from my own experience I think that his idea was that he had found meaning in it for himself. He had found it the way to growth of character, and above all, had known the sustaining grace of God in a new and deeper way. Having found this for himself, he could share his experience with others. This, like all the precious things in life, becomes richer as it is shared. He permitted God to guide and use his pain.

Through it all, if we offer our suffering up to God, we shall be led into a deeper fellowship with Christ. We follow a Christ who walked a blood-stained path over jagged stones to Calvary. He warned us that to follow Him we, too, must daily bear a cross. As we do that, we have a new and deeper sense of fellowship with our Master. To bear the pain of unjust suffering is our Christian "vocation," for "when Christ suffered for you, he left you an example, and you must be following his footsteps." These words from the pen of an early disciple are as true today as when they were written nearly two thousand years ago. We often forget them until tragedy grips us and the road becomes rough. Then we can awaken to our Christian "vocation" and gain a new and deeper sense of fellowship with Christ.

It all depends upon how we take suffering. To rebel against suffering, to look for no meaning in it, to boast that

"My head is bloody, but unbowed"

may be good histrionics, but it is poor religion. If we accept them as of God's hands and pray for His guidance in the use of them, then pain, suffering, disappointment, or tragedy may become for us the way of life. I found it so in prison, and wrote thus:

I offer Thee my pain to thank
Thee for bearing Thy heavy cross,
Seeking Thy courage which never shrank
From taking the cup of bitter loss.

I offer Thee my pain to share
With all who walk in burdened night,
Comrades of Christ, flouting despair,
A phalanx of shields with courage bright.

I offer Thee my pain to use
Within Thy great redemption plan,
Knowing all lashes and foul abuse
Fulfill the pain of the Son of Man.

I offer Thee my pain in trust
That it will not all fruitless be;
Planted in Thy heart it must
Bloom to life from sorrow free.

Let us pray:

Thou hast placed us, O God, on a road where the climbing is often hard and the trail bitter. We cannot escape the reality of the road. But we thank Thee that we need not walk alone. In Thy strength we find strength, in Thy light we find joy and courage and hope. Gird us by Thy power, we pray, that we may grow in Christian character, may be true comrades to others who walk life's hard pathway, and may wait with patience and hope for that turn in the road where we shall see the light of the eternal city before us. *Amen.*

Three Failures

I will follow you, Lord. But. . . . Luke 9:61

TO THE sensitive spirit no pain is more irritating than the sense of failure. The only thing worse than the sense of failure is to have failed and to be insensitive to it. This was the tragedy of the three men who came to Jesus as recorded in Luke 9:57-62.

One man came running to Jesus, his face and eyes aglow with enthusiasm, saying, "I will follow you anywhere." He saw that Jesus was on the way to Jerusalem. A great crowd followed Him. Perhaps He would declare His Messiahship there and set up a new kingdom. It was a great idea, a wonderful opportunity. He would join up.

But Jesus didn't answer in the way the man expected. Jesus had set his face to go up to Jerusalem. He knew He was walking a way that led to a cross. When He looked at this young man, He noted his fine clothes and soft hands. He knew he sought glory but did not know the meaning of sacrifice. So He warned him, bluntly, harshly, "Foxes have holes, the wild birds have nests, but the Son of man has nowhere to lay his head." To follow the Master was no easy road.

This man turned away, for he feared hardship. He turned away not knowing that he had missed life's greatest opportunity. It was his own loss. Only those who are willing to bear hardship for their ideals are of any real value to a marching army, to a great crusade. The Communists know this and accept only those who have been tried in the fire of sacrifice. We Christians ought to know it by this time.

The quick, discerning eye of Jesus saw the second man who came to Him. He saw possibilities of leadership in him to which the man himself perhaps was blind. Jesus wanted him in His group and invited him to follow. "But"—how different life would be if we did not interject that "but" all the time! "But he said, 'Let me go and bury my father first of all.' "

This was certainly a valid excuse in ordinary circumstances. He meant that he must go home and look after family responsibilities first, take care of his father in his declining years. Then after paying all filial duties to the full, he would turn his attention to the call of God. This excuse would be good almost any place in the world

44

and especially cogent in Judaea or in China. But Jesus had faced this issue Himself. He had left His home and had refused to forsake His mission and return to His mother and brothers. He was on the way to Jerusalem. He saw the cross looming before Him. He knew that all other loyalties must be subordinated to the one supreme loyalty of doing the will of God. So He replied in words that were harsh, demanding, almost blasphemous, "Leave the dead," the spiritually dead, "to bury their own dead; you go and spread the news of the Reign of God."

This man failed because he feared for his family. Family loyalties are good until they become the supreme loyalty. In old China they were supreme. Nepotism became the root of corruption, nepotism, and national weakness. Communism has seen truly that until national or party loyalties supersede family loyalties there can be no strength. Jesus saw that until loyalty to God becomes supreme over all other loyalties, God cannot rule in heart or home or country.

The third failure, like the first, volunteered to follow Jesus. He had noted the growing popularity of Jesus. He knew that He was marching toward Jerusalem. He had heard of His miracles. He sensed that something great was about to happen. A new kingdom might spring into existence. It would be well to be on the inside from the beginning. So he comes to Jesus jauntily, confidently, assured of a ready welcome, saying, "I will follow you Lord, but"—there is that "but" again!—"But let me first say good-bye to my people at home."

This man was a wise politician. He feared the lack of popularity. He wanted to be on the winning side. So he would go home, have a series of feasts for his friends, explain why he was joining this new crusade, and assure them that they could count on him to look after their interests. He wanted to keep his political fences in good shape. Then if this new venture should prove a failure, he would still be able to retreat without too much loss of face.

Jesus read his mind and could see his calculating ambition. He knew that he would be of no value in an emergency. When the going became tough, he would quit anyway. So with all candor, He refused him, saying, "No one is any use to the Reign of God who puts his hand to the plough and then looks behind him."

This is the story of the three failures as told by Luke. Fear of hardship, fear for the family, and fear of the crowd were the reasons for their failure to measure up to the demands of discipleship. These reasons for failure were not theirs only, but are often ours also. The tragedy was that they did not even realize they had failed. They turned away without any real regret.

Did the events of the succeeding weeks change their attitudes? I imagine them with the throng who went up to the Passover. See them mixing with the rabble that cried, "Crucify him! Crucify him!" Finally, hear their voices in the crowd that milled around the foot of the cross mocking in ribald laughter at the inglorious end of the Prophet of Galilee. One of them congratulated himself that he had not been duped by this strange dreamer into sacrificing his comfort for a bootless adventure. One reflected that he had been right in his refusal to flout his family in obedience to such radical demands. The third felt a glow of satisfaction that his hard, practical sense had kept him from offending his neighbors and friends to follow a lost cause. The three men knew that it was not *they* but Jesus who had failed.

For they saw only Calvary, and that on one day. They had no eyes for God's vindication of His Son in a glorious resurrection. They could not understand that history would confirm Paul's statement that in the cross is both "the wisdom of God" and the "power of God."

Let us pray:

We humbly confess, O Christ, that we are often like these three men who failed. We, too, would follow Thee to Jerusalem but not to Calvary. Often we first seek ease, popular approval, and our own family interests, counting them more important than

Thy kingdom. We are deaf to Thy warning that "he who would save his life must lose it." Forgive us, we pray, and may the shame of our failure go deep enough to bind us to Thee in a love and loyalty that follows even to the cross. *Amen.*

If You Have Faith

If you have faith . . . say to this hill. . . . —Matthew 21:21

THE BACKGROUND in China has not changed. If I could have escaped from that prison and gone to the foot of Mount Omei, the sacred mountain in the western part of Szechuan Province, I would have seen again, as I have seen in other years, the thousands of pilgrims toiling slowly up its winding, stony steps to its cloud-crowned peak. They continue to stop at each shrine, burn their incense, and get the seal of the local temple upon a piece of yellow cloth. Then they go on their way to the next temple. Thus, up and up they climb, taking two or three days to make the journey to the top, burning incense and paying their vows at all shrines and temples. They return to hang their seal-imprinted yellow cloth before the god of their homes as sure evidence of their faith, devotion, and sacrifice. This age-old hunger for God still burns in China.

The foreground has changed; youth now struts in all its brash sureness. Whatever else communism may have done in China, there is no denying that it has galvanized Chinese youth awake. One of the most heartbreaking experiences of yesterday was to go into country villages and see the number of young men wasting their days gambling and drinking in some tea shop, oblivious to China's tragic need of their help to rebuild society. The Communists have changed that. They came proclaiming a new faith and a new duty, declaring that old shackles of evil habit and social oppression must be cast off and challenging youth to join the marching crusade. Youth today in China is awake.

Today many Chinese youth are fired with a faith. It is a faith in the perfectibility of society and of man. It is a faith that the resources of science can be used to the full for the satisfaction of all man's real needs in a society in which all injustice is to be finally abolished. It is a faith that man can do this through his own strength alone. Yet it proclaims that in so doing man is not working *against* but *with* the universe. At the heart of all matter and of all historic change is a progressive development that will inevitably result in the perfect society. It is man's task to co-operate with this inevitable.

One day in prison I heard one of the government officials exhorting a group of young people who were going into government service. "You must learn the doctrines of Marx and Lenin, and know the fundamental faith of the Communist movement," he warned. "If you fail there, you will be swept away by the first wave of opposition. Only as you have the true Marxist faith can you stand against all difficulties."

All of this is stated in "scientific" terminology, and idealism is scoffed at and derided. To the Communists, God does not exist. But when he interprets history and projects his idea of change and progress into the future, he speaks in faith. He believes in the god of change though he spells God with no capital letter. He dreams of a Communist state that is similar to the Jewish messianic kingdom stripped of all spiritual connotations. The Communist, too, cannot move mountains except by faith.

Planted in the midst of this gigantic struggle in China is the Christian church. It is there like a leaven. It lives by its faith. The Christian church is a torch in a dark night proclaiming that there is a new way, an answer to all man's basic needs. As I studied the New Testament by a prison window and meditated upon the great themes of our Christian message, I was more sure than ever that in Christ, and in Him alone, we can find the sure word for our day.

Our faith is not something which we have invented or even

something which we have discovered. It is primarily God's revelation of Himself to us through His Son, our Lord. Man has an upreach, but before that there was God's downreach. The human element is in it; our blindness, our slowness to comprehend, our timidness in accepting, our failure to apply our faith to our own times. But in spite of our mortality and sin, God reaches out to us. He has taken the initiative. Through the life and teachings, death and resurrection of Christ, He has proclaimed His power, His purpose, and His undiscouraged love.

So the world today is a battleground of contending faiths. In China the conflict is sharp and clear. Perhaps we can put it this way:

> Up mountain steps sound melancholy tamps
> Of pilgrims' staff and feet that grimly seek
> In temple halls where Buddhist priests light lamps
> Before dark shrines, an answer that will meet
> Man's ceaseless quest for God. On plain below
> Youth's strong, derisive laughter blankets dread
> As together they would reap and sow,
> Scorning angry demons and gods now dead.
>
> Mary stands before a voiceless tomb,
> Bereft of hope until the Master's word
> Restores her Christ. Or to that upper room
> Comes one to grieving men, the Risen Lord.
> Vain is man's search for God in clime or clan
> Till He comes Himself, the Son of Man.

This conflict is not only in China. It is within our own hearts. We are tempted to follow false gods or to give way to that cynicism which renounces all faith. We are content to dwell within the stone walls of our secular prisons. But God will not leave us alone. In our grief we hear His voice. Into our fellowship of tragedy, need, and frustration He comes even though the doors be closed. We cannot shut Him out. He comes to us, the undiscouraged Lover, speaking to us through the voice of the Son of Man.

This is our faith, a faith that is not subject either to proof or disproof in scientific terms. But it is always open to verification as it is lived out in the daily round of our common days. With this faith, we are girded to meet the gigantic difficulties which face us today. Without it, we lapse into cynicism and despair and are swept away in the rising tide of the Communist movement or some other equally materialistic gospel. With it, we are sustained by the boundless resources of God. It is to experience what Jesus was talking about when He said to His disciples, "If you have faith . . . if you say to this hill, 'Take and throw yourself into the sea,' it will be done."

Let us pray:

Thy revelation of Thyself to us, O God, is a mystery beyond our understanding. It is the radiance that lightens our days. We comprehend but little of it. Our Father, may we do Thy will as we know it from day to day in the faith that as we accept and obey Thee, Thy light will guide us into closer fellowship with Thyself. Through Christ our Lord. *Amen.*

Our Christian Vocation

You must be following his footsteps. —I Peter 2:21

NOTHING SAPS one's moral vitality more rapidly than self-pity. To think that you are alone in your difficulty, that God has given to you a burden to bear that is not known to others, and that you can be sorry for yourself because you are a lone traveler upon the path of pain—this is to surrender to weakness, fear, and defeat.

On the contrary, when you realize, as I did in prison, that you are only one of multitudes who have been caught in the tragedy which stalks across our world today, and that many persons have faced more difficult trials than you—there is strength in such thought.

China is still in the throes of revolution. She is groping blindly, haltingly, but with persistent determination for a better way of life. The ignorance and sin of men, both those of foreign nations and of China, have added to the sum total of suffering and tragedy. Revolutions are never without their cost. My imprisonment was a small part of that cost.

To look at it in this way made my own imprisonment easier. I thought of the scores of missionaries who were interned during the Japanese war and waited through many months for a long-delayed release. I thought of Chinese Christians who had lost their all under the heel of a Communist dictatorship. I looked at the men there in jail with me. They had been arrested and brought to prison without any assurance that their families could keep from starving and had been kept there for months without any contact with those whom they loved. After their release months or years later, they would go back into a society where they had no job, no certainty of a livelihood. What is more serious, many of the Chinese prisoners had no sustaining faith, no confidence that this experience could be or would be used in a creative way. When I saw what they faced, certainly I had no reason to whine.

But we Christians have more than this. Not only do we see our suffering as one with others, but also we follow the Christ who suffered. We call ourselves His "disciples." Surely a disciple can expect nothing better than his teacher.

One early writer states that Jesus was perfected by suffering and that He "has been tempted in every respect like ourselves." Another writes that "when Christ suffered for you, he left you an example, and you must be following his footsteps." To do that is our Christian vocation.

I have never visited Nazareth where Jesus grew up. But I assume it is little different from thousands of Chinese villages. There the struggle for food and clothes is desperate. People live on a single street packed together in their shops which are also their homes. The thin partitions and gossiping tongues make all family problems public problems. Punishment of children is sharp and violent, providing a release for emotional tensions of over-worked adults. Dirt, disease, ignorance, and poverty turn life into a dull treadmill that deadens all finer feelings. Yet, this is the kind of town in which Jesus grew up. He well knew the petty irritations, the clawing fears, hates, and jealousies that are common to such a village. By some miracle which we cannot understand, He rose above the squalor, filth, and sin and blossomed forth into a life of such sensitiveness, purity, insight, and faith that men worshipped him as the Son of God. As we meditate on this fact and try to follow His footsteps, surely we have no right to complain of our lot. Think upon these facts, and self-pity evaporates.

Jesus also walked alone. It is true that He was never in solitary imprisonment as I. But even in solitary I knew that many friends were on the outside and some even there in prison who understood what I stood for shared with me in purpose and ideals. Though separated from me by prison walls, those outside were sharing with me in suffering. I was not alone in a real sense.

But Jesus was alone. No one understood Him. His family thought Him mad. The crowds forsook Him when He got into trouble. His disciples fled in a crisis, one of them even betraying Him. He had no one who really understood what He was talking about, who really shared in His purposes and dreams. To the very end, He walked alone. I think His walking alone must have been the hardest of all to bear. Thinking of that, I knew that the way that I was traveling was much easier than His; I dared not complain. I followed One who lived and worked and dreamed and suffered alone.

Let us pray:

Deliver us, O God, from the corroding acids of self-pity. Open our eyes to the tragedy and suffering common to all men, and to the gallantry with which so many uncomplainingly carry their pain. Make us ashamed of our whining. In courage and in patience may we accept our crosses and follow our Master to the end that the world may be redeemed and our own lives glorified through fellowship with Him in pain and in joy. *Amen.*

The Great Paradox

Whoever loses his life for my sake and the gospel's will save it. —Mark 8:35

OF ALL the teachings of Jesus, none is more difficult than His words about the cross. They dropped like a bombshell upon the ears of the disciples. The group had just acclaimed Him the Christ, the long-expected Messiah. They dreamed of Him as one who had power—who would defeat the Roman dictatorship, and who would establish the kingdom of Israel as an everlasting kingdom.

While their minds are filled with these dreams of power and glory, Jesus affirms that He must "endure great suffering, . . . be rejected by the elders and the high priests, . . . be killed." Peter rebukes Jesus for such tragic thoughts. Whereupon, Jesus says again, "If anyone wishes to follow me, let him deny himself, take up his cross, and so follow me, for . . . whoever loses his life for my sake and the gospel's will save it." The way of suffering and sacrifice is the way to life.

These words of Jesus left His disciples completely dumbfounded. They did not understand the meaning of what Jesus was saying. Power, to them, was always linked with material splendor. Go to Egypt and see the great pyramids. They were built at infinite cost of labor and life to perpetuate the memory of some monarch. That is power! Go to India and stand before that marvellous work of architecture at Agra. See how a king has enshrined his love of his queen into the most beautiful, and probably the most expensive, tomb in the world. You stand in wonder. That is glory! Go to Moscow and look upon that magnificent palace of the Tsars, now the seat of Soviet power. It is the nerve center for marching armies, secret police, nationalized industry, and of a monolithic

state. That is supremacy! These things the disciples could understand, as can we. But to talk of sacrifice and death, of loyalty and
love to the uttermost as the way to life—that is something which
is difficult to comprehend. They could not understand it.

Neither could they appreciate the truth of it. It is so much
easier to believe that life comes as we reach for it with greedy,
restless hands. It is easier to believe it will be ours as we give
rein to our selfish desires and claimant passions. Push others out of
the way and get what you want! That must be the way to life.
But Jesus says that it is not the way. We gain only as we give;
we have life only as we lose it. Joy and peace and fullness of life
are by-products of love and loyalty and sacrifice. That, Jesus affirms,
is God's way. That is the way the world is put together.

It is still difficult for us to see the power of this way. A man
with a gun always seems to have the power. Those guards in my
prison shouted out their orders, and we obeyed. The Communists
affirm that all democratic processes are so much eye-wash and that
revolutions can be accomplished only by marching armies and
ruthless dictatorships. To talk of tolerance, love, a free search for
the truth, and respect for personality as basic to any good government is to talk language they cannot understand. Unfortunately,
it is a language that we, too, do not understand too well. Even in
our "free nations" there are always those who have no more
faith in the way of freedom than do the Communists.

It is only in the light of the cross that the meaning, the truth,
and the power of this teaching of Jesus become dynamic. Jesus
did not just *say* this teaching and leave it as a pious exhortation
to His disciples. His teaching became an *act*, an act of such love
and total sacrifice that men saw in it the way of life. That act
gave to men a new dimension, a new understanding of God's
power and love. They saw the truth of God's relation to His world.
And they felt the power of that relation, the power to chasten
men's spirits, win their loyalty, and lead them to a dedication of
their all.

In a thousand ways, men have confessed the transforming power of the love of Christ as revealed in His death.

> Before Thy cross I bow in shame,
>   Hating my sins accursed,
> And by the power of Thy dear name
>   The chains of habit burst.
>
> From the cross Thy forgiving word
>   Rebukes my hate-filled heart;
> I know that love alone can afford
>   Safety from Satan's dart.
>
> Thy cross is as a bugle call
>   To rise and follow Thee,
> For only as I give my all
>   Can I Thy servant be.
>
> Thy cross is as a shining light
>   Upon the world's dark way,
> Warning all who strive for right
>   Must with their life-blood pay.

This love of Christ first touches you and me. But it cannot stop there. It is love's prerogative to share, and that sharing knows no boundaries.

Some years ago in India I met a young man who had seen the meaning of this. He was a college graduate who had become a load carrier. A number of summers at a mountain resort, where the foreigners gathered to escape the heat of the plains, had impressed him with the tragic life of the coolies who carried loads up and down that mountain. He felt their need so keenly that he determined to do something about it. So he, with his knowledge of English and his A.B. degree, became a coolie. Eating their rice and carrying their loads, he understood their lot. With his help they secured better restplaces and teashops, better wages and fairer conditions. And he, through his unselfish identification with them, discovered the truth of the Master's teaching that we gain life only as we lose it.

The road has not changed. It still winds up a stony way from Jericho to Jerusalem. It is still beset by thieves, still halts before screaming mobs and compromising judges, and ends at last on a bleak hill outside the city wall. It is the road of sacrifice. It is the road to life abundant.

Let us pray:

Forgive us, Master, that we so easily shrug off the stern conditions of Christian discipleship. We rejoice in Thy love. We bow in reverence before Thy cross and Thy unswerving loyalty to the way of aggressive goodwill. We exalt Thee; we praise Thee; we worship Thee. But we shrink from following Thee even though we know that in Thy way alone is life. Strengthen Thou our faltering wills and help us truly to follow Thee whatever the cost. *Amen.*

A Zest for Prayer

Maintain your zest for prayer. —Colossians 4:2

Even though he was in prison, Paul could write letters to his friends in Philippi, Colossae, and other places. I could write to no one. But if I could have written, I think that I would have made the same request that he made, that my friends maintain their "zest for prayer," and "pray for me as well." Many times I had a sense of God's sustaining grace that I could account for in no other way than that it had been made available to me through the prayers of others. I wrote:

Strange Gardener,
How do you grow fruit of such luscious taste
Amid the rocks and sands of adversity,
Or where persecution quivers over a desert waste?
Is there a secret spring we cannot see?

I believe that there is a secret spring. That secret spring is prayer.

It is strange, if we really believe in God, that we do not believe in and practice prayer more fervently. Since there is a God who created us, surely He did not seal off our minds so that He could no longer make contact with us. God cannot be more helpless than we. Even we can speak to one another. If God can make contact with us through the noise and hurry and earthliness of our daily lives, He can influence our decisions and guide our actions. This means that to believe that we can touch others' lives through prayer is not unreasonable. It is an inescapable corollary of the belief in a creative, loving, redeeming God.

However, our problem is not only one of logic but also one of habit. We must learn to pray. We never have taken the time to do so. We know that we cannot become efficient typists or skilled pianists without practice. But we somehow feel that we ought to drift into sainthood. When we think about it, we know that the only way to form a zest for prayer is to pray. As we pray, we shall grow to understand the need for prayer and the power there is in it.

We shall also come to understand the limitations of prayer. Christian prayer is always hedged about with one great condition, "But thy will, not mine, be done." It always seeks to put one who prays into right relation with God. Christian prayer seeks to make the one who prays understand the will of God in a particular situation. Then it makes the one who prays eager to co-operate with God in the doing of His will.

Many Christians do not understand this fact. Still fewer non-Christians know what we are talking about. One day one of the officials came to the door while we, squatting around our rice bowl, were eating. Looking at me, he said, "Stockwell!" I stood up. He said, "We do not permit anyone to pray in this prison." He then passed on, and I sat down. Another judge had said to me earlier, "We know that your wife is praying for you, but that's not going to get you out of prison."

I said nothing. To have got him to understand I would have

had to explain to him the whole Christian concept of prayer—it is so completely different from Communist ideas. The Communists think of prayer as some kind of magic incantation by which we try to change the will of God or the order of events. This is superstition, both to them and to us. They never dream that prayer is a way of placing one's life in God's hands, accepting His will for one's life from day to day, and finding, as one does this, a peace and joy, a patience and power that could come from nowhere else. To try to explain prayer to one who has never known it is as difficult as to describe the pungent scent of the Chinese "kwei-hwa" to one who has never smelled it.

If we pray with understanding, persistence, and definiteness, something happens. This is the reason that Paul wrote his friends to maintain their "zest for prayer," and then added, "and pray for me as well." He knew that prayer gains in strength as it becomes definite. If they would pray for him, then they might include also all the company of Christians at Rome, thus helping their prayers grow both in definiteness and inclusiveness. Through prayer God would expand their sympathies and enlarge their concerns. Both they and Paul would grow in grace.

It was that way with me in prison. Those months of imprisonment deepened my understanding and experience of prayer. I had no contact with the outside world that any official could check on. But I felt that the spiritual contact between me and my loved ones, between me and my Christian friends in China and around the world had been unbroken. The prison doors were locked on the outside, but they could not lock out the spirit of God. The realization of His presence and power was too real, too constant, and too satisfying to deny. I believed, and continue to believe, that my prayers for those who were on the outside and for fellow prisoners who were caught in tragedy and loneliness sustained them as their prayers sustained me.

There are doors locked on the outside
Bolting loneliness within,
Where dread and hopelessness abide
And pain of former sin.

There are doors locked on the inside,
Where men sit tense with fear,
Where blackest demons nightly ride
And white ghosts coldly leer.

There are doors locked on neither side
Wherein dwell safety and peace,
Where unguessed resources reside
Waiting creative release.

The Master can enter your door
By the secret way of prayer
Both joy and fellowship restore,
Give life beyond compare.

Let us pray:

We thank Thee, our Father, for the liberating experience of communion with Thee. We rejoice that we do not need to face life alone. Before its multiplied perplexities and burdens we are baffled, distraught, and helpless. But when we hear Thee say, "Come to me all ye laboring and burdened," we find the way to peace and creative living for ourselves and for those whom we love. May this be our bread and drink from day to day. *Amen.*

Desert Dialogue

So the tempter came up and said to him. —Matthew 4:3

NO PLACE in the New Testament is the sharp contrast between the Communist view of life and that of Jesus more clearly set forth than in the desert dialogue between Jesus and the devil. In each of the three conversations the answer of Jesus illuminates the difference between His way and the way of all materialism, Communist or capitalist. The devil says to Jesus:

> "He who would a leader be
> Must usher in prosperity
> Strike off bonds and make men free
> Of economic slavery,
> Turn the very stones to bread
> So the least are fully fed."

Jesus replied:

> " 'Tis true that we must feed the least,
> But surely man is more than beast
> Although each day he sits at feast
> From inner storm is not released.
> For man is also living soul;
> In God alone he finds his goal."

The issue is clear-cut; man must make his choice. The meaning of life is involved in the issue. The Communist says that all life is determined by the hunger for bread and by those who own and control the resources and tools of production. Put these into the hands of the people, solve your economic problem justly, and all other problems will solve themselves, says the Communist.

Jesus does not deny the importance of food. He only denies that man can live *by bread alone*. His own life was devoted to the meeting of men's physical needs—healing disease, feeding the hungry, and struggling for justice against the tyranny of Rome. The church has followed its Lord in this concern for human welfare—building hospitals, opening schools, and striving for social justice.

But Jesus saw the meaning of life as more than bread; therefore He went forth preaching the kingdom of God, the rule of God in men's lives. William Booth affirmed out of his lifetime of experience in the Salvation Army, "You cannot change a man by washing his shirt." Man's life is determined not only by the hunger for bread, but also by hunger for God. Life finds meaning only as it is related to this deeper hunger. So the devil tried a second time:

> "How can you trust your inner light?
> If you prove by marvellous sight—
> Leap from temple and safely alight,
> Or some such sign—that you are right,
> The world will flock to banner new
> And worship you as leader true."

Jesus replied:

> "The Spirit's way do you understand?
> That men change hearts is God's demand.
> Though many miracles startle the land,
> Our evils still will not disband.
> The one who safe in God abides
> Will know the grace that He confides."

Again the issue is clear. It relates to the way of life. Jesus sees that way as one of quiet faith, a life lived in fellowship with God and under the guidance of God. The inner voice sounds above the loud clamor around. The materialist, whether in China or in America, trusts in big parades, indoctrination by force, quick results that impress the masses, and finally, the power and glory which accrue to the leaders.

The way of Jesus is the way of patience, love, and humility. It is the faith in the freedom of the human spirit and the ultimate victory of God's way. The way of communism and of all types of materialism—and how easily we Christians succumb to its temptations—is the way of impatient intolerance, the forcing of outward conformities, the use of wealth and power to get quick results. One builds upon a rock; the other, on sand. And the end is the storm of war that sweeps all away in a flood of bloodshed, tragedy, and disillusionment. The road that Hitler walked yesterday men walk again today. We will not learn the way of life. The devil speaks for the last time:

> "If you would be a leader wise
> You must learn to compromise,
> Scale all ideals to common size,
> And each sharp issue then disguise.
> To kneel and worship the world's ways
> Is difficult, but always pays."

To which Jesus answers:

> "I would worship God alone;
> No such schemes would He condone.
> He challenges men His reign to own,
> All tribute bring to heavenly throne.
> This way may lead to Calvary,
> But I shall walk with spirit free."

Here again is the issue of the goal of life. To Jesus the goal of life was to do the will of God; the discovery of and obedience to that will was His life-purpose.

If you are a Communist, you have no questions about doing the "will of God." God does not exist for the Communist. The only truth is that which advances the Communist cause. What looks to us like a compromise, what we call "double talk," is always consistent—always consistent in the interests of advancing the Communist cause. The method used to attain the end does not matter. The only thing that is important is to attain the end, the victory of communism around the world.

I have used the word *Communist*, for that is the issue which thrust itself upon me in jail day after day. There I learned to understand communism more clearly and to hate it—the doctrine, not the people who are caught in its net of half-truths and falsehoods—more deeply than ever. But even as I saw how sharply it challenged the way of Christ, I knew that the same materialism in other forms challenges the way of Christ in America. The tempter comes to all of us, speaking the same language that he spoke to Jesus: insisting that God is not real, that our faith is but a fiction, and that our way of life is an empty futility. How we answer that challenge determines what we shall be.

Let us pray:

O God, deliver us from blindness to our own sins and the evils of our own society. The half-truths and blandishments of Satan are just as tempting today as ever. Always, we find it easier to discover the speck in another's eye than to awaken to the log which is in our own. Open Thou our eyes that we may see through the thin veneer, the shabby tinsel, the false façade of our own civilization. *Amen.*

The Power of Song

After the hymn of praise they went out. —Matthew 26:30

COMMUNISM WINS its converts not only through the logic of its reasoning but even more through the passion of its songs.

During the first long period of my imprisonment, I was at a center where the government was training its new cadres. The young people, seventy-five to a hundred of them at a time, were brought in and given six or eight weeks of training and indoctrination before being sent out to government jobs. The mornings were spent in study; the afternoons and evenings in singing. The leader had no instrument other than a pitch pipe. Sounding the note, he would sing off a phrase. Then the group would sing it over in the same way. Thus phrase after phrase was lined off until the young people had the melody firmly in mind. After that, they memorized the words. The tunes were catchy, easy to remember. One of the most beautiful tunes was built upon the theme of the second movement of Mendelssohn's "Italian Symphony," another on the "Battle Hymn of the Republic." Over and over they sang these songs until the whole courtyard rang with music. In this way the hates and fears, the hope and faith of communism sang themselves into the minds and hearts of these youth. What was done with this training group was repeated with the prisoners in their hour of singing each day. This is being done all over China: in schools, offices, army, and training groups. China is singing herself into the Communist ideology.

Whether the Communists learned this use of song from the Christians, the Greek Catholic Church of Russia, and the Protestant groups in China, I do not know. But it is certainly in the Christian tradition. We Christians got our first songs from the Hebrew Psalter, a book of hymnology that sustained the faith both of Jew and of Christian in many a time of trial. How much Jesus and His little group of disciples joined in song, we do not know. But their familiarity with the Psalter is beyond dispute. They closed the Last Supper together in Jerusalem with a hymn. Then they went out to face the terrors of the night.

This power of song is strange. I experienced it in prison. Having no hymnal, I made a list of the songs and hymns which I could remember. During my long months of solitary, I paced back and forth across my ten-foot cell room singing the great hymns of the church over and over again. My friend next door, the Canadian doctor, had no Bible or hymn book, but he had a retentive memory and a good voice. His morning and afternoon devotions consisted of hymn-singing. The French Catholic priest in the other room had no Bible or prayer book either. But I could hear him not only repeating the prayers that he could remember but also humming his Latin hymns. To all of us music came as a sustaining power.

I shall never forget my second Christmas in prison. My Canadian friend had gone. The French Father had been moved elsewhere. I was the only foreigner left in that prison, but I was not the only Christian. In the room next to me was a Chinese Christian of great faith, a faith that he sang forth with rich baritone from day to day. I did not know him. But on that second Christmas Eve he sang a large repertoire of Christmas carols for me. He sang arias from "the Messiah" and other Christmas music, closing with "Merry Christmas to you!" It meant much to me. A few weeks later, I was moved from that prison to another. As I left, I whistled the tune, "God be with you till we meet again!" I knew he would understand, for we spoke the same langauge. We worshipped the same Lord.

Whence comes this power of song? I do not know. Perhaps it is because faith never becomes real until it rises to song. There are depths and heights to Christian faith which cannot be put into words. There are overtones which always escape the net of prose phraseology. There are meanings that we may experience but that we cannot state. Only as we break into song can we begin to express the inexpressible.

Perhaps it is because song, like nothing else, grips our emotions. Emotions determine our actions far more than logical thought. A singing army is a marching army; it is a victorious army. A singing Christian is a joyous Christian and a convincing exponent of his faith in Christ. Whether it be Christian or Communist, no faith goes far in convincing others until it breaks into song. If we would win over the Communists, not only must we out-think them and out-live them but also we must out-sing them. The psalmist, reporting the goodness of Jehovah, writes, "He raised me from a lonesome pit, a muddy bog, he set my foot on a rock and steadied my steps, putting a new song in my mouth." No faith is complete unless it culminates in a new song. A singing faith is more powerful than an army with banners.

> You take the sword;
> Give me a song!
> The city we'll march around
> By music together bound,
> Raise victorious sound
> Till walls crumble to ground,

Yielding without a word
All entrenchments strong.
You may keep the sword;
Give me a thrilling song.

You take the law;
Give me a song!
Music gladdens hearts,
New ideals imparts,
To play sustaining parts
Against Satanic darts.
Evil may nearer draw;
It cannot stay for long.
You may rule by law;
I shall woo with song.

You take the wine;
Give me a song!
Singing we face the night,
Girded by courage bright,
Held by spirit's might,
Ready to die for right.
Music's lyrics fine
To heroes bold belong.
You may need the wine;
I shall sing a song.

Let us pray:

Send down Thy Spirit upon us, O God, until we not only live our faith but also sing forth the victory that is Thine. Grant us that upwelling spring of joy which sets all the bells ringing in our souls and glorifies the round of daily duties with the radiance of Thy presence. *Amen.*

Where Christianity Fails

Some sneered, while others said, "We will hear you again."
—Acts 17:32

SOMETIMES WE blame ourselves for failures when the failure is not ours but that of others.

Paul had fled from Berea to Athens where he spent some time waiting for his companions to catch up with him. In Athens he proclaimed the good news of God's revelation of Himself in Christ. From the brief summary of what he said as recorded in Acts, it appears that he preached well. He began where the people were, with their interest in religion, that interest evident in the multiplied idols on every side. He quoted their own poets with appreciation. He proclaimed that he had come not to destroy but to fulfill the best in their religious aspirations. The Athenians listened with appreciation. Then Paul set forth the ethical implications of the gospel and called upon them to repent. When he spoke of the life and death and resurrection of Jesus, they turned away. Some sneered while others said, "We will hear you again." His preaching proved a dismal failure. A few listened but not enough to establish a real Christian fellowship. We hear of other churches —in Corinth, Philippi, and other cities of that day—but none at Athens. Paul seemingly had failed.

But it was not Paul's failure. It was the failure of his hearers. God had spoken through him, but God could not get through the wall of indifference and hostility which the Athenians had erected. Paul found as Jesus had discovered earlier, that no matter how good the seed, it does not take root if the soil be hard, stony, and unreceptive. It fails in its purpose.

The Athenians would not listen, for to them religion was a philosophy to be talked about rather than an act to be lived. They were seeking a new philosophy that could be tasted like a new wine, appreciated and enjoyed but not seriously practiced. Our educated Chinese often complain that the New Testament is too simple.

It is different from the teachings of Confucius in that it is not abstruse, difficult to understand, and productive of long debate. It is clear, simple, and demanding of right action; therefore, the educated Chinese, like the Athenians, often turn from it.

Some years ago a group of us visited a magistrate in a county seat in West China. At the close of a delightful visit, punctuated with tea and cakes, the magistrate said, "I am not a Christian; my wife is. I am too busy now to study religion. However, I realize that all religions have good in them. Some day, when I have the time, I am going to study Buddhism, Confucianism, and Christianity—for, after all, religion is a mighty fine recreation."

This exactly expresses the Athenian mind Paul faced and the mind of many persons today. To them religion is not a bugle call to action, a challenge to nobler living, a power that transforms life. It is a philosophy which, like an antique vase, is to be set up and admired.

Neither did those Athenians feel any need of the wares which Paul was peddling. They lived on the surface of life, unconscious of deeper levels of agony, pain, and spiritual striving.

Many of the Communists in China today are living on the same level. Speak to them about religion, and they do not know what you are talking about. I think of that doggerel we sing:

> "Oh! the bulldog on the bank,
> And the bullfrog in the pool,
> The bulldog called the bullfrog,
> A green old water fool."

Of course, the bulldog living in a different environment could not imagine how the frog could find joy in the cool dampness of his retreat. But someday stark tragedy may grip the bulldog—or the Communist—by the throat and fling him down from his safe embankment, forcing him to discover that there are depths to life which his crass materialistic philosophy has ignored. Until that happens, he remains both blind and deaf to any religious appeal.

The price Paul demanded also was too high for the Athenians. How strange to Athenian ears this gospel of the cross must have sounded! Paul always lifted up the cross demanding that people understand it and accept it as their way of life. As Paul spoke of this, the cost of following Jesus, the Athenians turned away. They wanted a "free Gospel," a gift that would require nothing of them, that would challenge no loyalty or sacrifice. They wanted a bargain-counter religion, a faith that could be had for little or nothing.

These Athenians are gone, but their descendants are legion. Those who think of religion as a philosophy to be discussed not a life to be lived, those who have no sense of their own inadequacy and need, and those who are unwilling to pay the cost of discipleship are on every side. They have encased themselves in a hard shell of indifference. Having ears, they do not hear; having eyes, they do not see. On such soil the good seed of the gospel has little chance of taking root. The growth of the Kingdom depends not only upon God's gift of Himself in Jesus but also upon our acceptance of that gift.

Let us pray:

As the hard ground awaits the plowshare to pulverize its surface so that seeds may take root and produce rich harvest, so we await Thee, O God. The soft luxury and passing pleasures of the hour dull our ears to Thy voice. We easily grow a shell of indifference, selfishness, and isolation, which separates us from the tragic need of our fellow men and thus from Thee. We pray that Thou wilt shatter this shell. Break through the hard crust of our lives that we may no longer be sterile ground. Make us to come alive to Thee and to our brothers. *Amen.*

Christian Etiquette

Put on the apron of humility to serve one another. —I Peter 5:5

Invited to a Chinese feast,
Each guest seeks the lowliest place,
Vies with others to be the least,
Until the host with courteous grace,
With many a smile and bow polite,
Seats each one in balance fine,
Establishing his happy right
From lowest place to pour the wine.

The Pharisee stands on temple steps,
Vaunts his virtue and seeks to obtain,
In spite of all his unpaid debts,
The highest seat in heaven's domain—
Thus proving, under religion's banners,
He still has need to learn his manners.

PERHAPS IT is because the Chinese have lived so close together that they have made proper etiquette about the most important thing in life. Etiquette is the outward expression of an inner attitude which may or may not exist. That attitude is consideration for the other man's feelings and a proper subjugation of one's own insistent pride. It is the virtue of humility.

We westerners, aggressive, insistent, and individualistic, have the moral standards of the frontier. Honesty, hard work, and reliability seem to us the most important virtues. Perhaps they are when your nearest neighbor is half a mile away. We seem to think that to "blow your top" is our prerogative and a good way to let off surplus steam. But in China it is different. There people are crowded together. To live in peace demands a constant consideration of the other person's feelings. An angry outburst, the loss of one's self-control, is a sin of great magnitude. Such a person wins little respect in Chinese eyes. You cannot live together, much less serve one another, until you have "put on the apron of humility."

Humility is not only the way to service but also the secret of growth. As long as we can stand on the steps of our own lives and thank God that we are not as other men, secure in our prejudice, blindness, and self-satisfaction, there is no hope of change. Repentance precedes growth; only as we admit our faults is there any hope of our changing them.

The Communists see that; therefore they insist upon confession. Because it all is done under a ruthless, dictatorial compulsion, the confessions are often shallow. They are often but superficial attempts to conform to a new pattern. When confession is honest, denoting a real change in thought and attitude, it is transforming.

Once or twice a week we had our "self-criticism and mutual criticism" hours. Each individual in the group told what faults he had observed within himself and expressed his determination to eradicate them. Then each member of the group commented on this confession, either approving the confession or pointing out some other fault which the person had not seen and admitted. If the one who had made the confession humbly admitted that he had these other faults and accepted the criticism of the group, his conduct was approved. But if he tried to protect himself by claiming more virtue than others thought him due, he was condemned for his pride and urged truly to repent. All insisted that you cannot change a bad habit until you really see it as bad and repent of that habit.

So it was in prison; so it is throughout China today. If this emphasis upon the need of humility were as sincere as we wish it were and if it were carried on under the banner of freedom, it would be the most stupendous revival known in the world. Communism recognizes that no new society can be built without new people, and that new people cannot be created until, in humility, they turn away from the old.

Humility, moreover, is the way to God. Man is the victim of mortality, ignorance, and sin. Whatever his achievements, man is still bound by these limitations that distinguish the finite from the infinite. A few decades slip away and life as man has known it is gone. All the pyramids of Egypt or the tombs as beautiful as the Taj Mahal at Agra, India, may perpetuate a memory, but they cannot halt the gnawing tooth of time. Man's knowledge grows from more to more but each new discovery emphasizes his ignorance in other fields or opens to his view further undiscovered territories. The wise man is the humble man, for he knows that he does not know. Sin as selfishness, as greed for power, as uncontrolled passion, and as oppression of others is endemic in the human race. We have little to boast about. In the eyes of God we stand stripped of all our futile pretenses.

The Communist does not see this, for he knows no infinite that abashes his finite. He insists upon honesty in business and in government, for without that he cannot build a cohesive society. To lie is to sin against the "truth," not a revealed truth as given of God but the "truth" as embodied in the best interests of the Communist society. He feels no humility as he stands before his own ignorance and his own mortality. He believes that his own ignorance will be abolished as men continue to discover the secrets of nature and to apply science to society's needs. He knows that death is a fact that we face because we are animals, but we can do nothing about it. We do not talk of it. So it is possible—indeed, inevitable —if one is a Communist, that he can boast, "I thank Thee, O God, I am not like the rest of men." Of course, officially a Communist could not boast thus, for to him "God" is just a byword learned from a decadent society.

But it cannot be so for us. As Christians we not only see our evil but also see our evil in the light of God's love as revealed upon the cross. Before that love we stand humiliated. We repent of our sins out of an inward desire and not because of outward compulsions. God has touched the core of our being with His righteousness and His love. Such repentance creates new men.

Let us pray:

Lead us, O God, to true and fruitful repentance. Help us honestly to see ourselves and to repent of the wrong in our lives that we may become what we want to be. We know that we cannot worship Thee until we not only have surrendered our wills to Thy will but also are in love and fellowship with our brothers. It is not easy to forgive others or to seek their forgiveness. Gird us, we pray Thee, for this battle with self until the victory of the spirit is ours, until we walk in humility before Thee and in love with our fellow men. *Amen.*

The Tragedy of Judas

Then he . . . went off and hanged himself. —Matthew 27:5

JUDAS IS the only suicide reported in the New Testament record. This act, like almost everything else about Judas, is an enigma which we cannot fully understand.

We really know very little about Judas. He was the only disciple who was not a Galilean. He always must have been an outsider not quite accepted by the rest. He probably felt that.

John reports that Judas carried the money bag for the group and dipped into it for his own ends. John further reports that Judas betrayed Jesus in order to obtain the thirty pieces of silver. But it is difficult to believe that this was his ony motive. Surely that little group of disciples, living upon the generosity of the poor peasants among whom they moved, could not have had enough in the company treasury at any time to have provided any real temptation to a thief. If they were as careful in checking up on their treasurer as a Chinese group would be, he could not have stolen very much.

Some have suggested that Judas betrayed Jesus out of a desire to force His hand. He believed that Jesus was the Messiah with supernatural power. He believed that He would restore Israel. He conceived the plan to force Jesus to do just that. If Jesus were arrested by the Jewish authorities, dragged before their Sanhedrin, perhaps even taken before the Roman rulers, He would be forced to declare Himself and prove His power by God's miracle. God would interfere. The people would rise in His defense. The old system would crumble to ashes before the majestic power of God, revealed in His Messiah, and the Kingdom would come at last. So Judas saw himself not as a traitor but as one who was abetting the purposes of God. When Judas's plans crashed and Jesus faced the death of a defeated revolutionary, Judas went off and hanged himself.

Or, it may be that Judas was caught in a situation similar to that in China today. The children, embued with superpatriotism, are reporting on their parents and men are denouncing their friends and neighbors. They report all acts of disloyalty, of corruption, and of failure. Such reports often have little basis in fact. If the accused admits the crimes he is accused of and humbly accepts his punishment, he is restored to public favor. If not, he is condemned as an enemy of the State and is treated harshly.

In Jerusalem, as in China, patriotism flamed high. Jesus had said things which sounded disloyal. Some were saying that He must be a friend of Rome. The Sanhedrin had its spies out watching, questioning, and sometimes arresting those who might create difficulty. They had talked to Judas, asked him just what his Master had said, and had suggested that if Jesus could appear before some of their leaders they would clearup all suspicions against Him. So, Judas agreed to help them to the end that all misunderstandings might be clarified in a quiet way—thus aiding both his nation and his Master. He believed the officials would be just. Not until the act had been done did he see their treachery. In bitter disillusionment with his own blundering, with his nation's leaders, and with the whole tragic denouement, he went off and hanged himself.

Thus, at every turn in the life of Judas we can ask, "Why?"

Why did you do it, Judas, follow
The wandering prophet of Galilee?
Did he lighten your heart's dark hollow
Or a new world help you to see?

Why did you do it, Judas, stay
All those months with wandering band?
Was there something in the Master's way
That held you, too deep to understand?

Why did you do it, Judas, take
All that silver from crafty priest?
If following Him had been a mistake,
How could money help in the least?

Why did you do it, Judas, receive
The bread and wine from the Master's hand?
Did you not see He willed to believe
Love's last appeal you would understand?

Why did you do it, Judas, betray
The Master with duplicity's kiss?
Would you force Him to change His way,
Reveal God's power by some artifice?

Why did you do it, Judas, return
To gleeful plotters that money in vain?
Did your conscience sear and burn,
Taking all joy from your ill-gotten gain?

Why did you do it, Judas, end
Your life on tall tree's crooked limb?
Did you not know God's love would befriend,
Would forgive your treachery even to Him?

It is this last "why" which remains with us. Men do not commit suicide until all roads are closed, until they are pushed over
the precipice of hopelessness.

Bitter regret pushes them to such extremes. They repent without hope. I saw it in prison; I felt the tug of it. The Communist officials insisted that we must each one admit our evil acts and wrong attitudes. Some in deep remorse and with tears admitted that all the fault had been theirs. This was to "wash the brain." But such remorse may easily lead to hopelessness. It also may be unjustified. The evil which we do is only partially due to sin. It is also due to ignorance. We need to recognize the complexity of our motives and emotions. To know that the evil we or that others do is a compound of pride, selfishness, and ignorance, is to better understand that evil. The remorse is still present, but there is an understanding which keeps it from sinking into hopelessness.

For the Christian there is more to it than this. There is the conviction that God forgives both our sins and our blunders if we are sincerely sorry for them. Such forgiveness is not simply a blotting out of sin. It is a creative love that enables us to rebuild upon the ashes of our yesterdays in the confidence that God will accept us and hold us within His love. It is this forgiving love of God that Judas had heard Jesus speak about so often but which he in his own extremity failed to rely upon. Without this all turned black for him.

Let us pray:

Thy faith in us, O God, is a mystery. When we are hopeless, Thy undiscouraged love will not forsake us. We hear Thy voice, saying, "Get up, lift up your mat, and walk." When our zeal is flickering out, we hear Thee say, "Young man, I bid you rise." Before we loved Thee, Thou didst first love us. This mystery we cannot fathom. It is the light that illumines our days. *Amen.*

Mastering Impatience

They imagined God's Reign would instantly come into view.
—Luke 19:11

I NEVER knew what the expression, "doing time," meant until I was put into jail. The most difficult aspect of being there in prison was the terrifying slowness with which the hours passed. At times it almost drove me mad.

I tried to philosophize about it by remembering that "we live in deeds, not years." I even tried to put the unimportance of time into a bit of verse.

> Father Time is an eccentric fellow
> A codger who walks with capricious gait,
> When we are young and eager to follow,
> He saunters at a provoking rate;
> When we are old and too tired to run,
> He urges us on with youthful zest;
> Stands almost still before holidays begun,
> Then rushes us through them with no time to rest.
> Methuselah's age was nine hundred or more,
> But he left nothing that we can see;
> While light still shines from Galilee's shore,
> From One who lived only to thirty-three.
> Father Time, perhaps, laughs at us folks,
> Overvaluing himself being one of his jokes.

But in spite of my attempts to laugh it off, the problem of time was still with me. It was difficult to master my impatience.

The answer that Jesus gave to the impatience of His disciples was to call them back to their present responsibilities. They were on the way to Jerusalem. Their imaginations were aflame with visions of the new glory and power that would be theirs when Jesus ushered in His kingdom. "They imagined God's Reign would instantly come into view." They were impatient to have it happen without any more delay. Whereupon, Jesus tells them the story of a nobleman who went into a far country, but before leaving home, he gave to each servant a sum of money with the injunction, "Trade with this till I come back." He did not indicate when he would come. He simply laid upon them their responsibility and expected them to carry it.

During my long period of solitary confinement, I tried to keep my mind and heart upon the task at hand and not to worry about the future. Some days that was fairly easy. I tried to establish a definite regimen for the day. I began the morning with prayer and song and broke the long afternoon with another period of worship. For a long period I had my New Testament and paper and ink at hand. I spent the days searching my New Testament and writing articles and devotional talks. I had my watch, and it was a great help. I would work for an hour, then pace the floor for half an hour, then work for another hour. Thus the day slipped by fairly easy.

After being transferred to another prison, I lived with seven or eight other men in one cell. The time passed more easily here than it did when I lived alone. Here the days were regulated for us. Much of the time was consumed in discussion and study of Communist ways of looking at life. But here, too, I had to fight impatience. In the periods of quiet in the early morning or when I lay at night on the floor in my corner of the room, a sense of the long time which I had spent in jail would sweep over me. I wondered if I would ever get out. Time seemed to drag on forever. Only by force of will could I turn to the present day's duties and leave the future in God's hands.

Almost the cruelest punishment we had was the complete uncertainty. I had once read that the Communists insisted that their jail sentences were much wiser and fairer than those of the West because they were indeterminate. They did not keep the prisoner in jail so many years for a particular crime; they kept him until they felt sure he was reformed. Reading about it sounded good.

Experiencing it proved terribly difficult. How often I felt that if I could know just what to expect, know just when I would be released, I could plan accordingly. Without that knowledge, I built up hopes on the merest shred of actions or attitudes of the officials. Then I would have those hopes dashed to the ground. Whatever the arguments may be for it, an indeterminate prison sentence is certainly much more difficult than a fixed one.

My impatient heart continued to fight the battle with time. It was a long and bitter struggle. By concentration on the task at hand, the facing of present responsibilities, I would at times push the issue into the background. But any moment of relaxation and in the long night watch when all was quiet, the battle was renewed. To master my impatience was not easy.

The only way out was to place the matter in God's hands, to resign myself to His will. If I could believe that the issues of the present were in His hands, that He was in control, that He was using and would continue to use my experience for His purposes, I could win my impatience. Whether I was in jail or at home with my loved ones in America made very little difference as long as I knew I was in His hands. If I could believe this great truth and hold on to it in faith, patience was mine and the victory was won. It was a surrender that had to be made each day.

Would I have had it otherwise? At times, when the flesh was in the ascendant, I wished that I could open the door to the future and no longer have to walk by faith but could walk by sight. But when the Spirit was in control, I knew that my wish to tear the veil from the future was a childish whim. We grow only as we walk into the unknown by faith, believing that all things are in God's hands.

And so, with heart surrendered, we may pray:

> We thank Thee, Lord, we cannot see
> Far down the winding road of life;
> That in our hand there is no key

To fathom its strange storm and strife
Or open its locked mystery.

But faith in Thee we would renew
And labor till the night is here,
Working as Thy stewards true,
Eager that the Lord appear.

We thank Thee, Lord, we cannot know
Just when or how our day is done;
Since no such sight dost Thou bestow,
As men are blinded by the sun,
We walk in darkness here below.

But daily Thou dost give us power
To bear our loads through toil and pain
And though we see the dark clouds lower,
To trust in Thee and not complain.

Three Swords

All who draw the sword shall die by the sword.

—Matthew 26:52

I have not come to bring peace but a sword. —Matthew 10:34
He who has no sword must sell his coat and buy one.

—Luke 22:36

THE MOST difficult aspect of those days in prison was the indoctrination in Communist ways of thinking. What made this
most difficult was that their teaching was a mixture of truth and
falsehood, all of which had to be accepted as the truth. It centered
upon economic and international problems and not upon matters
of Christian faith.

My fellow-prisoners ranted at me by the hour, laying upon my
shoulders all of the sins of America. When they declared that
China had received nothing good from the West and that our total

contribution to China could be summed up in "bedbugs, syphilis, and opium," I knew that they were lying. But when they launched into an exposition of America as a war-making, imperialistic power, a capitalism which is driven by its lust for markets and natural resources to impose its will upon colonial areas, I knew that they were not speaking the whole truth but half-truths that hurt. We are fighting the battle against communism with a tarnished shield.

It is true that the United States did not impose its will upon China in the same flagrant imperialistic way in which some of the other nations did. We did have a treaty, though, which granted us any and all of the special rights which other nations had won in the imperialistic manner. We insisted upon our share of the fruits of brigandage even though we did not share in the venture. We did not force opium on China, but our ships carried their full share of opium to her shores. Our banking and commercial interests pursued their business with the same cold eye to profits that characterized business men of other lands.

When my fellow-prisoners insisted that democracy in America is a hollow mockery, a thin veneer hiding the complete control of American life by Wall Street and "the sixty ruling families," I denied it. But when they asked: "How many laboring men have you ever elected to Congress? how many laboring men sit on your city councils, or upon your school boards, or even upon your church boards?" I could think of few of them.

When they talked of race prejudice, I knew they distorted the truth. They spoke of lynchings as if they were daily happenings. They saw the Negro as an oppressed peon who is no better off than in the days of slavery. They know nothing about the progress which has been made, the distance the Negro has climbed during the past seventy-five years. But that prejudice against the Negro still exists. That the Negro does not have an equal chance in most areas of American life, and that we whites are terribly race-conscious—are facts I could not deny. I could but hang my head in shame. It is difficult to fight when you cannot do it with a clear conscience.

I know that the struggle is difficult whether one is in prison in China or is free here in America. We must labor for democratic ways not only in those countries that are under the heel of a dictatorship but also within America itself. We must struggle against the forces that make for war not only in other lands but also in our own, too. We must preach the brotherhood and equality of man both abroad and at home. Only as we contritely admit our own faults and strive to mend them can we honestly condemn those tyrannies that are oppressing mankind in ways beyond our knowledge and imaginings.

As I thought of America, I thought of the three times Jesus used the figure of a sword. He used it once at the time of His arrest in the Garden when He rebuked a disciple for cutting off the ear of the servant of the High Priest. His warning sounds out over the centuries, "All who draw the sword shall die by the sword." The way of violence is self-destructive.

We hate communism, but we cannot stop it by military methods alone. At best, the use of force is temporary, negative, a stop-gap method. It does not solve the problem. I can still hear my fellow-prisoners in that Chinese jail saying, "We Communists don't want war. But remember that the First World War produced a Communist Russia, the second a Communist eastern Europe and a Communist China. Give us a third and we will have all the rest of the world Communist except the United States, and it will be Fascist." How much truth there is in this I do not know. But certainly war creates those tragic areas of suffering and hunger and hopelessness which become the seedbed of communism. The way of war does not solve our problem.

> O America!
> Sheathe the sword of self-destruction!
> Quench war's greedy fire,

Lest its vengeance dire
Destroy the home of civilization.
Make an end of desolation!
Else ruthless Mars will sire
A cosmic funeral pyre,
Consume thee in its conflagration.

Another time Jesus used the figure of the sword was in His warning to His disciples, "I have not come to bring peace but a sword," or, as Luke puts it, "You think I am here to make peace on earth? No, I tell you, it is dissension." Jesus knew that men must make choices and that His challenge for men to see the truth and accept it would create division, argument, contention. Truth always does that. To see and speak the truth even in love is not easy. Truth always offends the prejudices or the selfish interests of others. The Communists twist the truth to fit into their own ends, forcibly indoctrinating others to accept only that which the leaders may determine is true. In democratic lands there are always those groups that would use communistic means to whip up that uniformity which they consider necessary for the support of the state. But such indoctrination is self-defeating. The free spirits of men demand a truth which is freely known and freely accepted. We have nothing to fear but falsehood, prejudice, and those half-truths which befog our vision.

O America!
Draw the sword of clean distinction!
Eschew all useless lies!
Let dauntless truth arise
To guide our groping generation!
From halls of education
Come patient knowledge wise
And unselfish love that buys
A fabric faith for our own nation.

The third use Jesus made of the term *sword* was during the closing moments of the Last Supper. Jesus and His disciples were about to go out into the night. Jesus felt the oppressive threat which hovered over Him in the darkness. He knew He faced suffering, and warned His disciples that they, too, must be prepared to sacrifice their all. Turning to them, He flings out that epigrammatic challenge, "He who has no sword must sell his coat and buy one." The disciples did not understand. They did not see that He was telling them that the time for conflict had arrived, a time when a soldier will sell his coat of comfort for the sword of sacrifice.

The Communists understand the necessity of sacrifice. By their evident willingness to sacrifice for their faith, they have won the respect of many who did not accept their philosophy. They have no illusions that the revolution can be won without discipline. This is hard-headed realism for them and for us. The world of tomorrow will be shaped by those who are willing to sacrifice their all to build the new day. The issue, whether in the time of Jesus or now, depends upon our measure of consecration, upon our willingness to exchange our garments of comfortable indulgence for the rough tools of sacrificial creativeness. The choice is before us.

> O America!
> Take the sword of consecration!
> Burn out thy selfish dross,
> And plant thy Master's cross
> On new peaks of dedication!
> Root out fear and trepidation!
> With love thy shield emboss,
> For from thy timely loss
> One day will flower thine own salvation!

Let us pray:

We thank Thee, O God, for our nation. We thank Thee for the sacrifice that has made her great, the devotion that has made her strong, and the loyalty to Thee that has made her free. We pray that we may accept these gifts of past generations as a sacred trust. May we not squander them. Others have labored and we have entered into their labors. Help us to enlarge and perpetuate that equality, justice, and freedom which is the dream of all good men, that life may be rich for us and for all men. *Amen.*

Our Christian Duty

To Greeks and to barbarians, to wise and to foolish alike, I owe a duty. —Romans 1:14

SOME DAYS when life in prison was a little on the blue side, I was tempted to regrets. I wondered if the investment of my life in China had been worthwhile, whether the whole missionary effort had not been ill-conceived. I wondered whether the isolationists, with their gospel of detachment and irresponsibility, were not right after all.

The trouble is that no one will abide by the rules of isolationism, least of all the businessman and the trader. However much we may be vexed at the misunderstandings and conflicts of the world in which we live, we have no way of preventing the cross-fertilization of cultures, the interchange of ideas and ways of life.

Let us take the matter of war as an example. We might put it this way:

> The Romans wrote with stylus point
> On heavy sheets of vellum scroll,
> For muscled hand and stiffened joint
> Were better shaped to warrior's role.
>
> The Chinese used a brush of hair,
> Lightly held in supple hand,
> Writing characters was talent rare
> Only a scholar could command.

This crude writing with stylus bold
Reveals the habit of warlike race;
But Middle Kingdom's culture old
Bows in hieroglyphic grace.

Roman legions march far today
In tank and plane, as armored men,
While China forsakes her peaceful way
To write her future with steel-pointed pen.

The invention of gunpowder is to the credit of China; the ways of total and destructive war, to the credit or debit of the West. Now we share them together.

So it is with all that we possess. Paul said, "To Greeks and to barbarians, to wise and to foolish alike, I owe a duty." He knew that the roads on which he traveled, the language he spoke, the peace he enjoyed, the law under which he lived, and the culture which he was trying to fertilize with Christian ideals were all a gift to him that he could not repay. This is no less true today. Take the gifts of any culture—Roman, German, Japanese, Chinese, Indian, or Arabian—and lift them out of the total complex culture that is ours, and the loss would be beyond compute. Each has given to the world its best. The result is a growing mosaic of wondrous splendor and beauty.

When one realizes this debt, one comes possessed by a sense of gratitude and responsibility. We went to China to give, but more than a score of years of living among Chinese Christian friends gained us much more than we gave. To have known another civilization, to have shared with Chinese youth in their hopes and plans for a new nation, to have sat in at the birthpangs of a new Christian fellowship with all its multiplied problems and opportunities, to have seen the spirit of God move over a group of worshippers, bringing joy and courage and new resolves in the same way that Spirit moves in other countries of the world—all this has been a gift for which even in prison I was humbly grateful.

Having received so much, we can but give of our best. We share all that we have—our new techniques, our inventions, our ways of life, our books and music. No "bamboo curtains" or any other barriers can keep these things out. It was amusing to hear the radio just below me blaring out its condemnation of everything American. It was being blared out over a machine which was built in America, broadcasted from a station which was almost one-hundred percent equipped with American-made apparatus, and operated by men who probably got their know-how from America. New policies in the East or in the West may temporarily halt the interchange of cultures and the free movement of ideas and techniques, but they cannot block them entirely. When we continue to share with the rest of the world in material things and to accept from them the gifts which they stand ready to give, we cannot place an embargo on our Christian faith. We must share that, too, and thus repay some of the debt we owe.

Deeper than this, we share our Christian faith because sharing is the very nature of our faith. Having received so much from God, we cannot refuse to share with others the good news of His love and grace. Whether they receive it or not is something that we cannot determine. You cannot force religion upon another people. In fact, you cannot force any ideas upon another people unless you have dictatorial power. Then you can indoctrinate by force, but such indoctrination may be a very superficial thing. Religion that takes hold of the hearts and lives of others can only be freely received as it is freely given. It is an interchange among free spirits of the best that they know and the highest they have experienced. Such spirit of sharing has characterized all Christian work at its best in China. The seed in this way has taken root and will grow.

In this faith I brush aside the regrets and continue to believe that the investment of the years in China has been worth all it has cost.

Let us pray:

We thank Thee, Lord, that we cannot live alone. Thou hast created us for fellowship. Thou hast led us to span the waters with our ships and join the continents with a shuttle of planes. Thou hast bound us together with a web of wireless so that we cannot escape knowledge of good or of evil, of tragedy or of triumph anywhere in our world. Thou hast compelled us to be citizens of the world long before we have learned to be worthy of such high calling. We pray for that sensitive spirit of Christ, for that heart that is open to all men and responsive to their needs, that alone can fit us for this great day. *Amen.*

A Word for the Discouraged

To run our appointed course with steadiness. —Hebrews 12:2

EVERY DAY was not alike even in prison. Some days were aglow with a sense of God's presence. Some new insight into the New Testament, some new fact of our Christian faith, some inner glow set the bells ringing and turned a common day into a mountaintop experience. Other days were flat; the struggle to keep from sinking into the morass of hopelessness was most difficult.

While thinking upon that fact one morning, it occurred to me that most people do not live their lives in the mountains but upon the plains. Here is where the crops must be harvested, the dams built, and the cities erected. It is upon the plains that men work and suffer and die together. The great masses of men do not live on mountaintops but upon hot, steaming, fertile plains. If they know the grace of God, they know it in the busyness of daily toil for life-sustaining bread. If they know the mountains, they know them from the valleys. After all, it is from the valley that the grandeur of the mountains are most apparent. The mountains do not seem so high when you stand on top of them or when, high above them, you view them from a soaring plane. Looking up from the valley to their gigantic masses of towering crags, one feels their majesty, their steadfastness, and their enduring peace. Living on the lowlands has its advantages if we can see them.

Such a philosophical attitude toward the emotional lowlands through which we must pass is not always easy to maintain. Here are two things which we can do. First, we can expect such periods of low pressure and prepare ourselves for them. We will not be caught off guard and taken by surprise. Second, we can find help to live through them by recalling from our memory other times when God's grace has blessed us.

> The mountain climber has no constant sight
> Of snow-clad peaks that shoulder azure sky;
> But trudging upward, gains a hard-won right
> On lower ridge to pause a breath and eye
> The boundless panorama, range on range,
> Cradled in God's cloud-misty coverlet;
> Girded by hope and ecstasy passing strange,
> He pays the trail's hard toll with no regret.
>
> Jesus at dawn on lofty, cragged spot
> With Moses and Elijah, heard God speak,
> And there gained that courage that faltered not,
> The courage to bear His cross to love's high peak.
> We, like climber, at each spring sparkling clean,
> May wisely pause for rest and fill canteen.

This memory of what God has done for us comes out of our own experience. It was so with Paul. His encounter with Christ on the road to Damascus and his memory of God's voice to him then never left him. He thought of it again and again. Every Christian has some memory of God's goodness and grace which stands out like a sentinel peak above the flat drabness of daily life. Such a memory sustains and encourages us when we are in need.

In prison I knew such hours. One day the inquisitor came to my cell to accuse me again of something which I had not done. I continued to deny it. Finally, he threatened me with a firing squad, stating that that was the punishment meted out to all spies in time of war. Looking him straight in the eye, I replied that I was ready to go. That moment I felt a divine undergirding of strength and courage that came from no human source. God was there, and I knew it. At another time I was completely at loss as to what to say before a judge. I did not know the answer. Clear as a bell, God said, "Say this, and this and this—and it will be enough." I did so, and the tensions wore off. I cannot explain it, but the memory of those times when God had met my need gave me courage to believe that He would never let me down. What the future held I did not know. I did know that the future was in His hands.

We do not need to rely only upon our own experience. The New Testament and Christian history are full of experiences of men and women who have walked through the same dark valleys we must tread. They have known the sustaining power of God and have recorded their experiences to strengthen our hearts. In writing to the early church, the author of Hebrews cites a great list of these heroes of faith. He is trying to bring courage and zeal to a church which has grown cold. After marching this great list of martyrs before us, men and women who have died for their faith, he states that they are now in the bleachers watching us play the game. In the inspiration of what they have done, we ought to "run our appointed course with steadiness." We ought not only to look to them but also to look to Jesus who "steadily endured the cross, thinking nothing of its shame." In gratitude to all those who have gone before, and most of all, in gratitude to our Lord and Master, we dare not quit.

Let us pray:

We thank Thee, Lord, for the thrill of the unknown. We know not what each day may hold. But we know that when we have sought to do Thy will and have committed all into Thy hands, Thou hast given us strength for the daily load, peace at heart, and the assurance that all is well. *Amen.*

Trail's End

You must not grieve for them, like the rest of men who have no hope. —I Thessalonians 4:13

NO SUBJECT is as carefully avoided as that of death. We try to hide the grim reality of it. Our friend does not die but he "goes west," "passes on," "slips away." The organ plays; we join together to pay our last respects before a flower-hidden casket; the undertaker whispers, "He looks so natural, doesn't he?"—no one wants to admit that the most certain, most universal event in life has happened. We know death is real, but we hate to admit it.

Is our hesitancy due to the fact that our faith in the resurrection is so weak? We say that we believe, but has that belief really gripped us?

Some years ago a group of my Chinese pastor-friends were talking about the matter of death. They admitted that they rarely preached upon the subject of Christian immortality, for they could not imagine heaven. Their minds as children had been filled with Buddhist pictures of hell or of the ghosts and spirits which inhabit another world. They had turned away from that superstition but had found no adequate imaginative picture to take its place. Perhaps that is true of most of us.

We cannot imagine heaven. The pictures of heaven which appear in the Bible, golden streets and angels with harps, are really pictures of the millennial city and not of heaven at all. They do not satisfy us, and we have found no adequate substitute. Yet, for Paul and for his contemporaries the hope of the resurrection was a very real one, sustaining courage and lighting the future with a glorious vision. Our imagery cannot be like theirs, but there are some things we can say. If heaven is the creation of our Father, God, the expression of His love and care, it will have certain essentials, certain characteristics.

Heaven will be a place of greater freedom. Here on earth we are hampered by the prison-bars of unfortunate circumstance and by our mortal limitations. We dream of doing so much more than we accomplish. We are cut off from our work when we are best fit to do it. Here on earth we are beset by ignorance and by our blundering mistakes. But in heaven we shall be able to express perfectly what we have done so imperfectly here. As Rudyard Kipling has expressed it,

> "They shall splash at a ten-league canvas
> with brushes of comets' hair."

Heaven will provide an opportunity for continued growth. Some who live their full three-score years and ten may feel that they have given their all and desire no more. But great numbers of people are cut off in youth or in middle life. They are just at the beginning of life. Surely to them any future life that is worth desiring must provide continued growth, development, and satisfying accomplishment.

Heaven must also provide fellowship. We speak of the "fellowship of the saints." Most Protestants have looked askance at the custom of prayer for the dead. But surely, if we believe in the continuing life of those whom we love, we cannot feel that death has broken all contact. The spiritual forces which have bound us together are stronger than death. To try to pierce the beyond by ways of spiritualism has been disappointing. But to know that those whom we have loved and lost a while are still near us, comforting, encouraging, and guiding—has been the experience of more than one humble Christian.

If we can clothe our thought of heaven in this way, it becomes more real. Then we can believe that the trail's end is but the beginning. Then we shall grieve for those who have left us but not "like the rest of men who have no hope."

This hope is built not only upon a more helpful imagery but also upon reason. It is a corollary of a Christian faith that believes in God as a God of love. To think of a manufacturer who expends his thought and resources in building a factory to produce machines which are only to be thrown upon the junk heap is to conceive the erratic, the insane. To think that God has created man, the crown of all His creation, and has with infinite love and care helped him to grow into some semblance of Himself, and then simply blots him out—to think this is to make Christian faith a farce. That, I think, is what Paul is thinking when he maintains in that great chapter in First Corinthians that "if Christ did not rise, your faith is futile." He is not stating that our resurrection is guaranteed because we are as good as Christ; therefore, as worthy of being raised from the dead. Rather, he is insisting that the same God who, in His love and power raised Jesus, is the God who has not changed in His relation to us. Our hope depends not upon our own goodness but upon God's goodness and unmeasured love.

The courage which without fear faces death does not come out of imagination and reason alone; it also comes out of experience. It is the experience of the continuing and abiding power of Christ in our lives from day to day. If God be real in our daily life, it is possible to believe that He will be real to us always. If you have known the touch of His hand and the sound of His voice in danger, sorrow, or perplexity—you have experienced an inner assurance that neither life with its uncertainties nor death with its forbidding certainty can ever destroy. Then in life or death you may walk without fear.

> Do not fear whatever life
> May hold of weal or woe,
> For through all its stress and strife
> The Father's love will show.

The violence of the stormy waves
That drives through sea's wild foam
Draws us nearer to Him who saves
And leads us safely home.

The agony of the cross of pain
That lifts our tear-stained face
Helps more fully in Him to remain
And trust His sustaining grace.

So whatever life may hold
Of famine, danger, or sword,
We may walk with spirit bold,
Trusting our risen Lord.

Let us pray:

We thank Thee, Father, that our hope for the future depends not upon our virtue nor our worth but only upon Thy love. We praise Thee that the sense of immortality may be ours today. We pray that Thy life within our lives may grow from more to more until the morning breaks and we truly live with Thee. *Amen.*

Barnabas, the Encourager

Barnabas . . . "Son of Encouragement." —Acts 4:36

BARNABAS MOVES on and off the stage of early church history like a stagehand at a Chinese theater. When a new stage property is needed on a Chinese stage—a chair, a fan, a pot of tea, or some other item—the stagehand simply walks onto the stage, delivers the object, and then walks off again. The play goes right ahead with no one paying any attention to him. So it was with Barnabas!

The first time we hear of Barnabas, he is at Jerusalem soon after Jesus ascended to heaven. The day of Pentecost has swept thousands into the Christian fellowship. They all were busy praying, testifying, and preparing their ascension robes for the day when

94

Jesus would return. They were living and eating together, but no one was doing any work. Barnabas observed that supplies were running short and that the whole enterprise might come to an inglorious end. Without saying anything, he went off to his native Cyprus, sold his farm, and brought back the money and placed it "before the feet of the apostles." He made no fuss about it. He simply knew that the play must go on. This was characteristic of Barnabas "Son of Encouragement."

When Paul came down to Jerusalem after his conversion, he found everyone suspicious of him. Paul tried to join the apostles, but they were afraid of him. Barnabas, recognizing Paul's worth and believing in him, took him secretly to Peter and stood guarantor for his good conduct. If Barnabas had not stepped into the situation, Paul might have been lost to the Chirstian movement.

Later, Barnabas went up to Antioch to help in a revival. The revival was much larger than anyone had expected. Barnabas went on up to Tarsus to get the help of Paul. He brought him back and put him to work. He knew that if he could move Paul on to the stage and give him his lines, he would play his part in a marvellous way.

The facts proved again and again that Barnabas was right. On their first missionary journey together, they had not traversed half the first island before Paul assumed the leadership. Barnabas was glad to have it so. Later, when Paul was reprimanded before the council at Jerusalem for preaching a gospel that was different from that of the apostles, preaching that Gentiles could become Christians without first becoming circumcised Jews, it was Barnabas who smoothed things over. Later Barnabas and Paul had their differences and Paul went off with Silas as his companion rather than Barnabas. Barnabas does not need to help Paul any more. Paul can depend upon himself. Barnabas turns to Mark. He helps him over a period of difficulty and thus saves for the Christian Church the author of our earliest Gospel. All of this is done without any fanfare. Barnabas, like an efficient stagehand, moves on and off the stage attracting little attention, but through his service he makes it possible for the play to go on.

Barnabas believed in men. He saw the possibilities in Paul, in Mark, and in others. He encouraged them, steadied them, and moved them into places where their God-given talents could be used in the largest way. Looking back over our lives, all of us can thank God for some Barnabas who has given a word of cheer and confidence which carried us over some difficult bit of the road. Very little cheer and confidence was given in prison. But several times fellow-prisoners and once or twice a guard gave me some word or smile that set the whole day aglow with joy and hope.

I remember a little pint-sized missionary lady from England who had been with us out in West China for a year or so. She went into a leper colony to minister to lepers' needs. She found a Christian man there who worked with her. She preached and served with such enthusiasm that she brought new hope to that whole group of lepers. Before she came, the lepers had been quarrelsome and jealous, fighting among themselves. Many of them felt that life was hopeless. She came to tell them of a God who loved them. The tone of that colony changed. Christmas became a meaningful and happy day. On the Friday evening before Easter, the local Chinese pastor and I visited the leprosarium to join in a Passion Week service. At the close of the service, we administered the Sacrament of the Lord's Supper. We served bread and wine to men whose bodies were so twisted with disease that they could not kneel at the altar, and whose hands were so deformed that they could hardly receive the elements. But their eyes were alight with new joy and hope. God had used this little English missionary as His Barnabas to them.

Moreover, Barnabas believed in God. He believed that God had infinite resources and could take any kind of a wreck and make it over again. Through His love and power as revealed in Christ, God could touch the motive springs of men's lives, making them to desire goodness and strong to achieve it.

The Communists believe men must be changed. They talk of mutual responsibility, of a new society which men can build together. They try to awaken men's hatred of all groups that may stand in their way. The Communist state is the equivalent of our heaven, a heaven on earth, while all capitalist societies are little better than hell. So they preach. So they plead. So they threaten. They accomplish some results in changing men's attitudes. But it is not the Christian way.

The Christian way depends upon the love of God as revealed to us in Christ and made concrete to us by those who, like Barnabas, move on and off the stage of our lives, helping us to realize our own potentialities. To play the part of Barnabas is something each one of us can do if we have enough concern for others, enough faith in God, and enough sense and humility to stay out of the limelight.

Let us pray:

For all those who have touched our lives and helped us to be better, we thank Thee, O God. Without the help of others we would have failed. Grant that we in our turn may strengthen others, giving to them some of the joy and encouragement and hope which others have given us. *Amen.*

The Meaningfulness of Life

For the fulfilment of the prophetic scriptures.

—Matthew 26:56

JOY, HOPE, AND COURAGE may be found in pain only if that pain has meaning. During those long months in prison, I discovered that if I could believe that the whole experience would fit into the economy of God for the growth of Christian character and the redemption of the world—then my heart was at peace. Without that faith I would have gone mad. Some of my fellow-prisoners who lacked such faith lost their reason and tried to commit suicide.

The guards were always on watch for such extreme cases. Others bore the long ordeal with stoical indifference, accepting it as one accepts a drought or a flood.

One old man lost everything he once had had; wealth, political influence, and military power. He sat repeating his Buddhist scriptures with his body motionless and his lips moving. He had been warned that he was not to carry on such superstitious practices there in jail. But one day, when the rest of the men were out of the room for a minute, he turned to me and said, "They tell me not to repeat my Buddhist scriptures. But they don't understand. Without a religious faith there is nothing that holds life together." My faith and his faith were different, and I believe that mine was more adequate than his. But what he said is profoundly true. In the midst of suffering, without faith life falls apart.

Jesus knew that great truth. He started with a faith in God, a faith which He had learned at home. At His baptism and in the days of struggle to know the will of God in His desert experience, He saw His own relation to God and God's purpose for His life in clear outline. He chose a road that led to the cross. As he moved along that road, He felt Himself a part of the whole purpose of God as it had been revealed in the history of His people. We do not know how clearly He saw each step of the way, nor how much He realized what His sacrifice would mean for the redemption of the world. But He knew with full certainty that He was moving within the purpose of God. This certainty helped Him face the mob with courage and serenity on the night He was arrested in Gethsemane. He believed that it all had happened "for the fulfilment of the prophetic scriptures." If one can believe this, believe his life is in harmony with God's will, he can face anything.

I have often stood on the bank of one of those West China rivers, watching the turgid, surging current bearing along its burdens as it swept downward toward the far-away sea. In my prison cell I thought upon the different ways in which men accept life. It seemed to me that I saw it depicted on those West

China rivers. To the cynic life is but driftwood, meaningless and purposeless. To the determinist it may have meaning but that meaning cannot change things or help. Like a log caught in the mill-race, we are caught in the clutch of circumstance and swept down, willy-nilly, to the lumber mill below. The man of faith is as a cargo boat. In life he finds meaning. For him life has freedom, a limited freedom, but still enough freedom to permit him to co-operate with God in the achievement of high ends. To believe this is to find a meaningfulness to life without which all suffering is unrelieved blackness.

I tried to put these three alternative views of life into a few lines of verse:

> Life is but driftwood afloat in the river,
> Thrown into the stream by an unknown hand,
> By unseen forces pulled hither and thither,
> Helpless to meet man's real demand,
> Till caught in the grip of whirlpool's might
> It's sucked into vortex of dawnless night.
>
> Life is a cedar cut from the hill
> And cast into the swift-flowing stream,
> To be swept down to the waiting mill,
> There to be sawed into board and beam—
> A victim of man's economic state,
> Helpless to change its destined fate.
>
> Life is a boat loaded with cargo
> That follows the river's winding ways,
> But aided by sail and current's flow
> Moves steadily forward through sunlit days.
> Though rapids and storm delay its arrival,
> The Hand at the helm assures its survival.
>
> Life sweeps along on the stream of time,
> And no one escapes its surging power,

But whether it speaks of purpose sublime
Or is meaningless tragedy, dark and dour,
Depends upon a Spirit supreme
Who reveals to man a transforming dream.

There is no way of proving by any scientific process that one of these ways of life is right and the others are wrong. This cannot be proved any more than you can prove that love is better than hate, goodness better than evil, or trust better than doubt. The only proof is in the experience itself. We can only know as we practice, find for ourselves which way leads to life.

This experience, I believe, was my greatest gain from the long period in prison. I saw in the lives of other prisoners that cynicism and despair were suicidal. I noted that the spirit of resignation to a blind fate may give a certain courage to hold on but brings little peace and no joy. I knew in my own life and saw in a few others that creative faith which accepts suffering as something to be used of God, a meaningful part of His divine purpose. To accept it thus, as in some measure a "fulfilment of the prophetic scriptures," is to find meaning in it. From this springs joy and hope and courage—assets of inestimable value.

Let us pray:

We would not pray, O God, that the bitter cup of pain and tragedy be removed. We pray that we may see Thy will in it, may be given courage and strength to drink it. Through it all may we find our way to a closer fellowship with Thee. *Amen.*

The Upper Room

The disciples had gathered within closed doors for fear of the Jews. —John 20:19

WHEN WE speak of the upper room, our thoughts leap to the story of Pentecost, the story of the disciples gathered together awaiting the descent of the Holy Spirit. But there was another upper room—or perhaps the same room six weeks earlier. It was a different room, not because the place or the furniture was different, but because the spirit of the same men who had gathered there before was different. John reports they gathered there "within closed doors for fear" of their enemies. Those doors were shut.

> The doors were shut against men's fear
> Of Roman guard with sword and spear
> Who would drag all plotters bold
> To torture racks and dungeons cold.

> Within, men sat in dry-eyed grief
> That vile treachery, like a thief,
> Had stolen their hopes, and leader slain
> On savage cross of blood and pain.

> The sting of hatred filled their hearts
> At Pilate and priests who played their parts,
> An innocent man to callously slay,
> Hurrying to be done before Sabbath day.

> They bowed their heads in guilty shame
> That they who sought both power and fame
> Had, in a crisis, cravenly fled,
> Deserting their Master in helpless dread.

> The doors were shut, but One came in
> Who dispelled the night of fear and sin,
> Revealed Himself in person bright,
> Sent forth new men as heralds of light.

All were in that little room—fear, frustration, hate, and shame—emotions which tear our lives to pieces, drive us to deny our manhood, and lead us to do craven things of which we dare not speak.

They all were there, too, in my prison cell. Fear was so real that you could touch it. Some poor fellow would make a blunder—step into the hall without making the proper report, or approach a guard without saluting. The guard would shout, and the poor fellow would freeze in his steps. He would stand there for ten or fifteen minutes while the guard poured out his fury upon him in a tongue-lashing which left the poor fellow cowed and beaten. Or the shouts and bitter railing of a crowd of men who were engaged in the public trial of some unfortunate person would come to us through the paper-thin partitions of the prison. It was not our trial, but we cringed in sympathetic appreciation of the terror that gripped the victim.

It all seemed so hopeless. The lad who slept beside me was there because he had tried to end it all. He was working with the kitchen force and in a moment of despondency tried to take his own life. Again and again a wave of frustration swept over him and he would weep. Others noticed it and tried to force him to tell his worries; he refused to speak. How could he tell us of a small country farm, of birds and freedom, of friendship and work and the respect of others, and the love of mother and father expressed in the simple round of a peasant home? He wept for these things, things which had been long denied him and that he seemed so hopeless of knowing again.

Hate was in my prison cell, too. It was shadowed behind closed lips and guarded glances, but it was there. It flamed out of the guards' words and actions, hatred against those whom they must control and whom they had been taught to consider the enemies of the people. Hate begot hate. If the prisoners had been free to act, there would have been an explosion. But they had to smother all such emotions. To express even a bit of such emotions was to wear leg chains and handcuffs day and night until the spirit was broken.

Shame also was there in prison. The Communists believe in shame. They believe that there can be no change of attitude until men are ashamed of what they have done. They are right about that if the shame be honest. However, in prison it was not honest. A professed shame and the parading of acts long done become a hollow pretence. Yet, it was the only way to freedom. The shame of lying and deception was added to all other shames; men lived out days that they hated.

Fear, hate, and shame were all present in that upper room long ago. They were all in that Chungking prison cell. And they are buried deep in the hearts of men the world around, tragic and disruptive of all that is good.

The doors were shut but One came in whose presence changed all who were in the room. Just what happened none of us can tell. But the real presence of the Risen Lord was there. He changed everything. He brought victory out of defeat, changed hatred into love, failure into success, and loneliness into companionship. All the emotions which had gripped that small group and had held them prisoners were swept away. He struck off all the fetters. They were free men, free in the knowledge of God's presence, power, and forgiveness.

Some argue for a physical resurrection; others argue for a spiritual one. If the spiritual be more real than the physical, as we Christians insist it is, it would seem to me that to argue for a physical resurrection is to argue for a resurrection which is *less* real than the spiritual rather than *more* real. Just how it was, none of us can ever know. Paul says that it was a "spiritual body," which is probably as good a description as any. The essential fact is that the presence of Christ was real. Christ was real enough to change that upper room into a new upper room, a room of Pentecost and power, a room of spirit-filled men, a room where men had met the Lord.

Then, and now, that miracle is believable only as it is re-enacted in our lives. I, too, have seen hate, fear, and frustration give way to love, confidence, and hope. In that prison cell I felt the presence of the living Christ, as real and as transforming as He alone can be.

Let us pray:

O God, Thou knowest our deep need. Prejudice and hatred

plague us. The dark fog of discouragement wraps us round. The cold grip of fear and worry clutches at our hearts. We stand helpless and alone until we see Thee. Come Thou, O God, to open our eyes that we may behold the heavens filled with Thy chariots and horsemen. Come, Thou, in the quiet of the morning time or in the long night hushes, to whisper, "It is I, have no fear." *Amen.*

The Christian Hope

The day is almost here. —Romans 13:12

PAUL AND his contemporaries had one resource for the meeting of suffering and tragedy which we have largely lost today. That resource was their faith in the immediate return of Jesus.

One has but to leaf through the New Testament to see how brightly this hope flamed in the heart of the early church. The earliest letters of Paul to the church at Thessalonica center upon this theme. Later Paul may have felt that the return of Jesus would be postponed longer than he had first thought, but he never lost grip on this central and sustaining hope. The parables upon watchfulness in the first three Gospels record both the words of Jesus and the faith of the early church in this hope of Jesus' return. The faithful steward must be alert to his Lord's return. The stirring vision of John on the island of Patmos, though recorded in symbolic language, is clearly a call to courage and sacrifice, based upon the assurance that Jesus would quickly return to defeat the forces of evil and to establish His beneficent rule. Like Paul before him, John on Patmos believed "the day is almost here." The Gospel of John, probably written at the turn of the century mutes this apocalyptic hope and begins to reinterpret the physical return of Jesus as a spiritual indwelling of the living Christ. The book of Hebrews tries to revive the flagging spirit of a church that had grown cold in the faith, but no longer places the major emphasis upon the immediate return of Jesus. The church was beginning to lose some of that urgency of time under which the first generation of Christians lived.

We may regret this, but for most of us it is a fact that we cannot escape. I tried to put the contrast in this way:

Christians once knew time's urgency,
For they were sure the day was near
When Christ in glory would appear
As long foretold by priest and seer.
As faithful stewards in hope and fear
They eagerly waited their Master dear,
For they had great expectancy.

Christians have lost time's urgency,
We look at history in a different way,
Study fossils of ancient day,
Listen to what our wise men say,
Conclude our earth unchanged will stay;
For His return we seldom pray—
For we have little expectancy.

Awaken Thou us to time's urgency!
That we may have in hours' swift flight
A fleeting chance to reflect Thy light.
Come Thou in some vision bright
To show when men battle for right,
Christ is there in sustaining might—
Restoring our lost expectancy.

The spirit of timeless patience is not the tone of the New Testament. The tone there is that of the football gridiron, with the ball resting on the ten-yard line and two minutes to play. There is an urgency to living. All are on tiptoe, for Jesus is about to return. Such a hope put courage into burdened hearts. It moved as a cloud by day and a pillar of fire by night before the eyes of men who walked the road to martyrdom. To have abandoned this hope is no small loss to the Christian fellowship. Do we have anything which compensates for this?

To millions of Christians today the sense of an abiding, living Christ is just as real—indeed, more real than a physical return would be. One, of course, does not exclude the other. But with the rediscovery of "the Jesus of history," many find a more satisfactory Christian faith in the thought that,

> "The healing of His seamless dress
> Is by our beds of pain,"

or, that of

> ". . . Christ walking on the water
> Not of Gennesareth, but Thames!"

We often find it easier to speak of "the living Christ" than we do of "the Holy Spirit." It makes little difference, for the meaning is essentially the same. The important thing is that Christ becomes real to us, real as Companion, as Leader, as Lord.

This reality must be not only in relation to an inward sense of release and power but also in relation to the social issues of our day. Someone has defined communism as "organized impatience." Christianity should be no less an "organized impatience," impatience with all wrongs and injustices and prejudices that shut the door against Christ. Our Christian faith should gear into the society in which we live so closely that every achievement in winning for men their rights as sons and daughters of God would be for us a real second coming of Christ—not tomorrow, but today.

Communism is in a sense the conscience of our world today. It is lifting up the wrongs which exist and forcing us to look at them. If we will not right them through the love and sacrifice of the Christian way, communism will attempt to do it through a dictatorship. Time is running out. Perhaps God is warning us through the tragic tensions and bloody threats of these days that "the day is almost here." It can be a day of unrelieved darkness in which all that we hold most dear goes down in holocaust of war and atomic destruction. Or it may be a day when Christ will march into the minds and hearts and relationships of men and nations, reigning in love and power and bringing to all mankind new hope. The choice is ours.

Let us pray:

Waken us, our God, to the urgency of these days. May we see Thy judgment upon us for our sin as Thy challenge to us to build for justice, freedom, and peace. May we have the assurance that Thou art with us in all creative effort to make Thy will regnant in human life. May we believe that the kingdoms of this world may become the kingdoms of our Lord and Master. To that end, help us to labor in faith, in love, and in hope. *Amen.*

Winning Your Soul

He will be saved who holds out to the very end.
—Matthew 10:22

YEARS AGO I heard a sermon on the text, "In your patience ye shall win your souls." (ASV.) I forgot what was said, but the text stuck in my memory. I did not understand how patience and winning one's soul had much relation to each other until I got into prison. Then experience combined with further study of the New Testament opened my eyes. It is patience under suffering that wins one's soul. In Moffatt's translation our text reads, "He will be saved who holds out to the very end." Or, as Luke reports it, "Hold out steadfast and you win your souls." In both Matthew and Luke this assurance comes at the end of a long warning to His disciples in which Jesus states that they will face suffering and trial, be dragged before governors and kings, and will be subjected to ridicule and scourging because they are Christian disciples. If, they hold out in patience and courage, they will win their souls.

This means that under the test of suffering you discover what Christian resources you really have. I did not feel when I was arrested, nor do I feel now, that my Christian experience and faith were different from that of others. Mine is an ordinary garden variety which has nothing special about it. But it was enough to carry me through. The problem with most of us is that we are not put into those situations where we are under great strain. When we are, we find that our faith really works if we will use it. Thousands of humble Christians in China today are finding that their Christian faith does sustain, strengthen, and comfort them far more than they had dreamed possible.

Under such testing, one's faith grows. An unused muscle becomes flabby. Use it and it becomes hard and strong. Persecution and difficulty strengthen Christian faith in the same way. Probably many people wonder how the church can survive under a Communist dictatorship. They fail to realize that most of Christian history has been written under dictatorships of one kind or another. Jesus was born and lived under one. This is an old story to the Christian pilgrim. It is the kind of thing which Jesus expected would happen. But He knew that persecution rightly endured would not destroy but would strengthen the Christian fellowship.

It is strange, but that is just what happens. There were times in prison when I was stripped of everything. Then God moved in with His rich resources. He opened up new ways of thinking and living and gave me a deeper sense of His abiding spirit. It seemed to me that He isolated me from all other helps, as a scientist isolates his experimental material in a laboratory, until I could know that what I had came from Him and from Him alone.

Here, too, is where the sustaining power of God moves into our lives. We know the grace of God in proportion to our sense of felt need. When everything else is stripped away and we realize our own utter helplessness, then we throw ourselves upon God with a new completeness, a new abandon. God takes hold. That, certainly, was my experience. I knew, that if the day came when I would be freed from prison and the pressures of it all were off, then I might no longer have as keen a realization of God's presence as I had felt in prison. That would not be because God had forsaken me or because I had lost my faith. Rather, it would be because I would not be so sharply aware of my own helplessness. But never again shall I doubt God's power to sustain through long periods of pressing need. His enfolding presence is ever nigh.

All of this is possible if we have faith. By *faith* I mean more than an intellectual acceptance of the Christian way of life. Faith is broader than that. The faith which will sustain must be clear-eyed, an understanding acceptance of the great essentials of the Christian revelation. It must be a faith in which we know the reality of abiding in the Vine, have an experience of prayer and God's indwelling spirit. It must be a faith that includes the dedicated will and the flaming passion to share with others this wonder of God's love that has been known to us through Christ Jesus. Armed with this kind of faith, the Christian pilgrim can walk with patience the hard road of suffering, and so win his soul.

> Though bitter the bite of the stony trail,
> And frigid the winds that angry wail,
> Against the pilgrim they naught avail
> If clear be vision of holy grail.

> Though dark the trail across mountain wend,
> And black the valley below the bend,
> 'Tis joy our life's last breath to spend
> When held in the grip of a faithful Friend.

> Though road be long and progress slow,
> Days weighted with sorrow and nights with woe,
> 'Tis thrilling to front such stubborn foe
> To share with others the inner glow.

Let us pray:

We thank Thee, our Father, that Thou hast set us in the school of Christ. We find here the thrill of growth, of discovery, and of achievement. Help us in patience to face all difficulties, and through the strength which comes from Thee win through to life more abundant. *Amen.*

Thy Will Be Done

But thy will, not mine, be done. —Luke 22:42

AS I LIVED through those months in prison, I realized that it really did not make much difference what happened on the outside. It was what was happening on the inside that counted.

To put it in other words, if I could accept what had happened to me as the will of God for my life, I could face the worst with a certain equanimity, a gallantry of spirit that was otherwise impossible. It was to sing George Matheson's two great hymns, "O Love that wilt not let me go," and "Make me a captive, Lord"—to sing them, believe them, and act upon them.

To pray, "But thy will, not mine, be done," is not to believe that everything which happens is God's will. I do not believe that God put me in prison. My imprisonment was due to sin and ignorance, and to hate and fear. These things are as far removed from the will and spirit of God as daylight is from dark. God does not create tragedy, sorrow, loss, and pain. Much of it comes from man's own sin, both individual and social. Some comes from causes we do not know. But certainly God does not will evil for His children.

Looking at the matter in this way, we can say reverently that not even the crucifixion was the will of God. God did not will that His Son should die on a cross. He did not will that men should hate and lie. He did not will that men should be filled with jealousy and fear which leads them to do terrible things to their brothers—so terrible that we hardly dare think about them. Such was not His will.

But God did will the love that flamed in the heart of His Son, the love that flinched at no sacrifice, the love that led to the proclamation of His word at Jerusalem, the love that stood silent before

110

His accusers, the love that prayed in agony, "Father, forgive them." As Jesus thus expressed the spirit of the Father, He found a way through the cross to speak forth the love of God more persuasively than through any other act. Then men saw that cross not as an isolated act in the life of a martyr but the suffering love of God for each one of us here and now.

The prayer of Jesus in Gethsemane, "But thy will, not mine, be done," must, if we are true followers of our Master, be our prayer in our Gethsemanes. Only thus can we transform a blind fate into the providential goodness of God.

To accept imprisonment or any other accident of life as the will of God is to accept it as something which can be used of God. It is to believe that "prisoner of the Communists" can be transformed into "prisoner of Christ." It is to look up into the face of God and say, "Why this has happened to me I do not know. But I believe that Thou canst use it in Thy divine economy. If I could see through divine eyes, I would understand. If I could think not in hours or days but in centuries, I would see how it fits into the whole pattern of life. I cannot do that. I cannot see the meaning, but God can. Therefore, I accept it, believing that God can transmute it into Christian character and use it in some measure for the redemption of mankind."

To accept my imprisonment as within the will of God was to find that I was not alone. This was not a new road which I was travelling but a well-worn one. It was a road that has been worn by the feet of many martyrs, one that has been bloodstained by One who carried His cross. To believe this was to escape the most devastating of all emotions—self-pity. Some would deny the fact of suffering and thus rob our faith both of its cross and of its crown. But those who see truly must lift up the cross and proclaim it as the way to life. In this experience I could reach out my hands and touch many others who walked with me.

As I accepted those days of loneliness and uncertainty as the will of God, I found in them not only meaning and fellowship but also a sense of God's sustaining power. Someone has defined the "grace of God" as "God in action." I discovered it to be that power that changed my heartache into joy, my darkness into light, and granted me a certain buoyancy of spirit for which there was no other explanation than the "grace of God."

I continued to pray, sometimes haltingly and fearfully, sometimes with greater courage and faith, "Thy will, not mine, be done."

Let us pray:

> Forgive us, Lord, that we should seek
> To trust our own dust-blinded eyes,
> Unmindful of our vision weak,
> Lacking that sturdy faith that cries,
> "Thy will be done!"
>
> Forgive us, Lord, we seek to read
> Our future fate in crystal ball,
> Not trusting to Thy hand to lead,
> Nor praying that in dangers all,
> "Thy will be done!"
>
> Forgive us, Lord, that we still fear
> To cross the choppy sea with Thee,
> Knowing whenever Thou art near
> Our deep desire must always be
> "Thy will be done!"
>
> Forgive us, Lord, that stubborn will
> Would wrench our lives from Thy control;
> Pray Thee, our hearts Thy spirit fill,
> That we may pray, mind, heart, and soul,
> "Thy will be done!"
>
> *Amen.*